Dark Knights 3

The Dark Humor of Police Officers

The Laughter Continues

Robert L. Bryan

VU Jasper Campus Library
850 College Ave., Jasper, IN 47546

Copyright © 2019 Robert L. Bryan All rights reserved First Edition

Printed in the United States of America

For my parents. Gone for many years but never forgotten!

CONTENTS

Introduction……………………………………………..7

1:     Integrity -The Cornerstone of Policing…………..12

2:     First Police Action……………………………...……19

3:     Subway Bathrooms……………………………….23

4:     Room with a Surprise……………………………34

5:     In the Bag………………………………………….37

6:     When You Gotta Go – You Gotta Go……………41

7:     Combat Reloading……………………………...46

8:     The Organ Grinder……………………………….48

9:     The Dirty Magazine Store………………………..55

10:     Bumpy……………………………………………..62

11:     Ring Around the Rosie (or the Booth)…………..65

12:     Chief Stories………………………………………69

13:     On to the Academy……………………………...72

14:     A Day in the Country…………………………...77

15:     The Unreachable Star…………………………….79

16:     Can't We All Just Get Along…………………….82

17:     Next Stop – Siberia……………………………..85

18:	The Chief is a Bully	89
19:	Sgt. Bill's New Shoes	94
20:	I'll Get You for This	98
21:	I Love a Parade	102
22:	The Soda Man	106
23:	Happy Cyrus Day	109
24:	A Little Hungry	116
25:	Pasty Boy	121
26:	The Captain is Crazy	127
27:	It's a Piece of Cake	131
28:	Put in my Place	136
29:	Hee Haw	138
30:	The Duty Captain	143
31:	First Impression	146
32:	The Afterlife	149
33:	Passing Over	153
34:	Spinning Plates	155
35:	What Experts Say	161
36:	Afterlife Case Studies	164
37:	The Afterlife as an Afterlife Job	168

38:	The Merry Mailman……………………………….172
39:	The Longevity Penalty……………………………177
40:	Man With a Plan……………………………………179
41:	The Greatest Retirement Perk…………………...182
42:	There's No Place like Home………………………184
43:	Do You Miss the Job?..186

Introduction

A few years ago, I made the decision to become an author. My goals were realistic. I wasn't declaring myself a world-famous author – just an author. Even with such a modest avowal, to be an author I still had to write something. So, what would I write? When I began researching the literary world, a piece of advice for new authors I would come across over and over again was to write what you know. That made sense to me, so the question became - what did I know? My entire adult life had been spent in the field of law enforcement and security. I was a Border Patrol Agent for two years on the Mexican Border before returning to New York City and completing a twenty-year career with the New York City Transit Police and NYPD. I retired at the rank of Captain, and am currently the Chief Security Officer for a division of a New York State government agency. Additionally, I have a bachelor's degree in criminal justice and a master's in security management and I am an adjunct professor for two New York Metropolitan area colleges in Homeland Security and Law Enforcement studies. With this background, it was fairly simple to decide the major topics I should write about. The next problem, however, became selecting something specific to base a book on.

Police Officers perform a dangerous and usually thankless job. The physical dangers have always been and always will be a part of the occupation. What has increased dramatically, at least in my opinion, is the danger from within. If an accountant makes an honest mistake by entering a nine instead of a one in a ledger, the mistake is corrected and the accountant is told to be more careful. When a cop makes an honest mistake, even if his or her intentions were good, the line forms very quickly to destroy that police officer. The media, progressive social groups, the officer's department, and the district attorney quickly condemn the officer's actions before all the information is even known. I guess the best expression of my feelings of being a police officer in today's society is the fact that I am extremely happy that my son chose a career in the railroad (Shameless self-promotion alert - see my book, CONDUCTOR). Don't get me wrong, I have soured on the unfair conditions and scrutiny cops have to work under. I will never sour on cops. Police officers are heroes, and I thank God that there are still some of the best young people this country has to offer who are willing to endure being put under the microscope by the very large and vocal anti-police forces in society.

  Back to my dilemma. What about police work should I write about. I just stated my opinion of cops being heroes, but even if I had some heroic tales to spin (which I don't), I would be very uncomfortable writing a "Look at me – aren't I great." Besides, there are too many of those type books already on the market. I was looking for something different about cops to be the subject of my book. The question became – take away the characteristics of actual police work, and what do cops have in common? The light bulb illuminated above my head and I had my answer. Cops are funny. Without a doubt, the funniest stories I have heard throughout my life have been told by cops. What makes these cop tales so hysterical? I believe it is because the stories are usually irreverent and dark. The subject of a story may be a tragedy, and yet the cop can bring out something darkly funny about the incident. I believe this propensity toward dark humor is a necessary defense mechanism in law enforcement. Police officers tend to see people at their worst, when they are in the middle of a crisis or tragedy. Cops see death, sickness, injury, crime, mental illness, and danger on a daily basis. Internalizing all these negative interactions is a recipe for disaster. Look no further than police suicide statistics to understand what I mean. So, I say to hell with political correctness. Cops can be absolutely brutal to each other in their dark humor, and I sincerely hoped that hasn't changed. The ability to be dark, irreverent, politically incorrect, and taboo within the police world is, in fact, therapeutic.

Ok, enough time on the soapbox. Back to my police book. I decided to write DARK KNIGHTS, which traced my career through a series of funny (sometimes darkly funny) stories about the cops I worked with throughout the years. I had no great expectations for the book. In reality, it was really a test of the self-publishing process to understand everything necessary to publish a book, like cover design, manuscript format, book description, keywords, and promotion. So, I succeeded in getting Dark Knights published while learning from my numerous mistakes along the way. It was now time to focus my energy on writing something with more substance than funny cop stories. But then, a strange thing happened. Dark Knights actually began to sell. Don't get me wrong, it won't be on the New York Times bestsellers list anytime soon, but since it was published, it has remained on the Amazon best seller lists in all its categories.

What do you know? Maybe there is a market for funny cop stories. If Dark Knights was a success, it would stand to reason that another similar book would also be successful, right? But could I stay with the same theme, yet write about something different. Wait a minute. Before my police career in New York City, I spent two years as a Border Patrol Agent on the Mexican Border. The stories in the Border Patrol are just as dark and funny as any in the NYPD. But my time on the southern border was many, many years ago. I sat for weeks scratching out notes of my recollections on the border, but at the end of the day, I could recall nowhere near enough material for a book. Then, a stroke of luck in the form of a cardboard box. I was in my attic looking for something for my wife, when I stumbled upon this box that I had not seen for years. In it was every document I had kept during my time with the Border Patrol. I was amazed at how much material I kept. I had my daily training schedule from the academy, the roster with the names of everyone in my academy class, every report I wrote at my duty station, newspaper clippings, and photographs. As I went through these materials the memories began flooding my brain. I immediately abandoned the search for whatever I was supposed to look for and instead began furiously writing notes. Several months later, DARKS KNIGHTS 2 – BORDER PATROL EDITION became a reality.

Dark Knights 2 has also maintained a steady stream of sales, so it does not take a genius to float the idea – hey, what about Dark Knights 3? Even though it was a logical question, I did not see any way to do it. Essentially, I had shot my load of funny cop stories in Dark Knights. My humor magazine was empty. So, it was on to different projects. As Dark Knights began to circulate, however, I began to hear from more and more cops I had worked with throughout the years. The conversations were all very similar. They would tell me how funny they found the book, but they would then bring up some story and ask why I didn't put that particular incident in the book. After a while I began keeping track of these conversations/texts/emails. Most of the time my response to these revelations was "You're right – I completely forgot about that." What was the result of enough of those "I completely forgot" statements? - Dark Knights 3. I hope you enjoy.

Integrity – The Cornerstone of Policing

Integrity - the quality of being honest and having strong moral principles; moral uprightness.

Integrity – it's an important word in the law enforcement profession. Because society has placed police officers in a position to have dramatic impacts on the lives of the citizenry, and in some instances, to actually take life, integrity become the cornerstone for behavior. Despite certain media portrayals, during my career, I never saw integrity as being a problem in police work. Just the opposite. The officers I worked with and supervised routinely exhibited the highest levels of integrity. Nothing is ever one hundred percent, and in the NYPD, where there was an average of forty thousand uniformed members of the service during my career, you are always going to find some rotten apples in an orchard so large.

Right out of the gate, however, during my police academy training, I was exposed to some interesting characters that stretched the definition of integrity. During the first week of recruit training, we received our integrity lecture. A superior officer from the Inspectional Services Division made the rounds of all the recruit companies and explained all about integrity and corruption. The recruits were told all about grass eaters and meat eaters. A meat eater was a dirty cop who was dishonest by nature and who's actions on the job revolved around corrupt and illegal acts. A grass eater, on the other hand, was basically and honest cop, but with the right opportunity and motivation would commit illegal acts.

When my career began, I was a transit cop, and I went through the Transit Police Academy. I always believed that corruption issues were less relevant for transit cops, not because transit cops had more integrity than their NYPD brethren, but because the transit policing environment was less conducive to corruption. Think about it. Transit cops were not routinely entering homes, making large narcotics seizures, or making car stops – all areas where integrity could be put to the test. Of course, the Transit Police was not without organized corruption, but it was on a transit scale. I once knew of a transit cop who got arrested for "hand collecting." This cop would proceed to his steady post during the morning rush hour and disable the turnstiles. He would stand at the open slam gate and provide exceptional public service by accepting the tokens of the riders who were now unable to use the turnstile. He simply streamlined the experience by removing the middle man. If a rider did not yet have a token, there was no need to stop at the booth to purchase a token. This magnanimous cop gladly accepted the cash at the gate. What I found fascinating about this case was how stupid or comfortable a person can get with their corruption. This cop was hand collecting for several months before he was caught. How long did he seriously think it would be before someone thought there was something funny about the cop collecting the tokens and cash and reported it?

Back to my academy training. I learned about the grass eaters and meat eaters, and how I would be fired, jailed, and face eternal damnation if I took a free cup of coffee from a subway vendor. The lecture had its desired effect with me. I was not going to ever take one off center step. Then, my social science instructor entered the classroom. He introduced himself, his background with the department, and what the discipline of social science was all about. It was a great introduction. I still remember how he explained the three academic disciplines in the police academy as a hamburger. He said that police science was the meat and law was the bun. Social science, he said, was like ketchup. The whole thing just tasted better with the condiment. It was a brilliant analogy. A cop had to know the law and procedures, but it all went down better if you knew how to deal with people, which was what social science was all about. The instructor even had a handout. What a great, prepared instructor, I thought, to bring his own handout material. Then the handout reached my desk. What? I was looking at a catalogue for all types of jewelry. It seemed that our instructor also had a side business selling jewelry, and being a savvy entrepreneur, he recognized his recruits as a new customer base.

About a week later, at lunch time, I noticed a group of recruits surrounding a vehicle parked at the curb just outside the academy gate. My classmates and I investigated and found another instructor doing a land office business out of his trunk selling all kinds of Transit Police t-shirts. So much for eating grass. So much for eternal damnation.

Without a doubt, the most meaningful lecture I received regarding corruption during my academy training was provided by my police science instructor, and it was unofficial in nature. During one class, the subject of corruption came up, and he laid it out very succinctly on the blackboard. He first estimated what a police officer's average salary would be over the next twenty-year period and wrote that total on the board. Then he noted the average life expectancy and calculated the amount of pension benefit the average cop would collect during a lifetime. He then put a value on a lifetime of health insurance and put that number on the board. Once he had listed all the salary, pension and benefits a cop would receive during a lifetime, he totaled them all up and circled the final number. He then turned to the class and pointed to the final number. He said that if we were ever offered a bribe, and it was more than this number – take it! Otherwise, it's not worth it. You would never find this lecture in a corruption training lesson plan, but in some bizarre way, it made sense.

I met many unique and interesting characters during my twenty years with the NYC Transit Police and NYPD, both members of the service and civilians. These characters fill many pages in my books. The first individual who made an impression with me was Police Officer Charlie. Charlie was a tall, sturdy affable Irishman who was in my recruit company in the police academy. I hate to promulgate stereotypes, but Charlie liked to have a drink occasionally. Okay, maybe a little more than occasionally. Charlie was single and lived in an apartment above an Irish pub in the

Rockaway Beach section of Queens. Most weekends during recruit training, Charlie would hold court in his apartment, which soon acquired the nickname of the "action house." The residence may well have been called the debauchery house. Thank goodness, I wasn't a very social person at the time. It wasn't until the last few weekends before graduation that I began frequenting the action house. I don't know if I would have survived any more than a few action house sessions.

    After graduation, I didn't see Charlie for quite some time. I was assigned to the Tactical Patrol Force in Queens for six months before being transferred to District 4 in Lower Manhattan. Charlie was assigned to District 33 in the East New York Section of Brooklyn. The next time I ran into Charlie was about two years after coming on the job. It was during an in-service training session at the Transit Police facility at 300 Gold Street in Brooklyn. It was refreshing to see that Charlie had not changed a bit. There were a couple of cops present from our old recruit company and during a break, just like old times, Charlie held court with a story.

    Charlie told of marching in the previous St. Patrick's Day Parade. There isn't a cop in New York City who doesn't know about the parade, both working it and marching in it. After the parade there is a big party sponsored by the Patrolman's Benevolent Association. The party is supposed to be the concluding event of a festive day, but as many cops know, it was actually the kick-off event for a very, very long night. So, Charlie related how after the parade he attended the party and began having a few beers.

Sometime during the afternoon, he met a very pretty Puerto Rican girl, and they immediately hit it off. Charlie said that this girl was not a cop, and that he really did not know where she came from. Charlie said that the afternoon flowed, along with the beer. Mix in a few shots, and Charlie admitted that when darkness enveloped the city, he was completely shitfaced.

Charlie emphasized that he was a responsible drinker, so he had not driven to the parade. He went on to say that his inebriated state did not complicate his transportation problems because his new fried nobly volunteered to drive him home. Charlie said that the evening was extremely hazy, but that he remembered slouching in the front seat of her car, and noting that they were not heading towards Rockaway, but appeared to be driving north, in the opposite direction. He said that he also remembered his new friend commenting about taking a drive in the country before going home. Charlie stated that his next recollection was being out in the woods, being led by the hand along a dirt path by the girl. At a clearing, Charlie said that she turned and basically jumped him. Clothes were strewn all over the bushes and it was game on. Charlie said he awoke naked, on his back, with first touch of dawn working its way through the leaves of the tree above him. As his senses returned to him he saw that his friend was already completely dressed and appeared to be moving on the dirt path.

Charlie said "Hey, where are you going?"

The girl responded, "I have to go, baby. My husband gets up at sunrise."

Charlie said he filed away the husband comment for future reference, but that he had more immediate concerns. "Hey, the sun's coming up in a few minutes. Isn't it a little late to worry about your husband?"

"Not if I hurry. I live around the corner."

Charlie said his head was pounding, partially from the alcohol and partially from trying to make sense out of what was happening.

"Sorry, I have to go." She said as she disappeared down the path.

Charlie said he was still completely naked as he began to follow. "Wait a minute. How am I supposed to get home?"

As dawns early light illuminated the scene, clarity began to set into Charlies' brain. It may not have been good, but he understood his situation. The drive to the country really had not been that far. Charlie was standing in his birthday suit in the middle of a vacant lot in the South Bronx. While he stood there stunned in all his glory, daily New York City life was taking shape around him, with kids walking along the sidewalk carrying schoolbooks and a Sanitation street sweeper cleaning the street. Charlie said he had to run through the lot to find all his clothes and then take the subway home to Rockaway.

First Police Action

When I graduated from the police academy, I was assigned to the Tactical Patrol Force in District 20. TPF was an impressive sounding name, but the reality was that it was a unit that had been resurrected from the past to have an army of rookie cops riding trains throughout the city between the hours of 8PM and 4AM. Talk about your plum assignments. Before I could get into this prime unit, myself and all my classmates had to receive two weeks of field training. Since my TPF unit was housed in District 20 in Queens, our field training was conducted in District 20. Nowadays, police departments have units devoted specifically to field training programs for newly graduated officers. In 1982, the Transit Police Department's idea of field training was to spread the rookies out amongst the regular district personnel for two weeks. This was an especially bad idea in District 20 where the average cop had over fifteen years on the job and detested the idea of having to babysit one and sometimes two rookies at a time. It was even worse on midnights where most of the cops already had twenty years on the job.

To be kind, let's just say that most of the steady midnight cops in District 20 were creatures of habit who were set in their ways. The problem was that their ways did not really center around police work. To the uninformed civilian, it may appear that most of the nighttime protectors of the city were most concerned with getting a good night's sleep. I found out this prime directive very quickly.

When I graduated the police academy, there was not much time to revel in the pomp of the ceremony. I was assigned to work a midnight shift the next day which meant that I had to be in at 11:25PM that same night. That first midnight roll call was filled with classmates who had graduated earlier in the day. The veteran District 20 midnight cops were horrified and did not try to hide their disdain with having their world rocked with our presence. I was assigned to work with Police Officer Joe. Joe had twenty-one years on the job and had worked midnights in District 20 for the past ten years. All I will say about that first night on patrol was that at least Joe was not a phony. He didn't try to mask his disgust at having to drag me around with him. He never introduced himself, and at the end of the roll call he departed the command without a word. I ran after him and said, "I think I'm with you tonight," to which he responded by grunting and continuing walking down the platform.

Let me explain how much of a drag I was going to be on Joe. We were assigned to patrol four stations – 179th Street, 169th Street, Parsons Blvd., and Sutphin Blvd. This large a post would seem to constitute a considerable dragging effort on Joe's part. The reality, however, was that we proceeded directly to 179th Street and to the front end of the

Manhattan bound platform. I followed Joe about twenty feet past an employee's only swing gate and waited while Joe fumbled with his key ring. A moment later he opened the door of a room and we entered. It turned out this room was an old tower that was no longer in use. It was the perfect bedroom for Joe. Without saying a word, he stripped off his coat, gun belt and bullet proof vest. He laid down on a large cushion that was spread out on a table and appeared ready for a night of blissful sleep. Before the sand man took over, I had to ask a question. "What should I do?" Joe's answer was terse and to the point. "Do what you want, but I'm going to sleep."

What was I supposed to do now? I certainly wasn't going to curl up next to Joe. This was my first night on patrol as a cop. This is where I began to change the world. But here I was locked in this dirty room while Joe got his beauty sleep. The door to the room had a small peep hole from which I could view the platform. So, I stood with my eye pressed against the peep hole, hoping that maybe something would happen that would allow me to take my fist police action. Maybe I would see someone get robbed or assaulted, or at least someone writing graffiti on the platform wall.

About an hour into my surveillance I observed a middle age male walk down the steps onto the platform. There was no train in the station at the time, so the man hesitated momentarily on the platform before walking in my direction. I assumed he just wanted to be in a position to board the first car of the train when it arrived, but to my surprise, he continued walking through the employee's only gate and right up to the door I was peeking through. He couldn't see me, but I was staring right at his face. What the heck was he doing? Then I heard what sounded like water hitting the door. Wait a minute. I know exactly what he's doing. He's urinating on the door. I sprinted across the room and shook Joe's arm. His annoyed tone was obvious. "What? What?"

"There's a guy pissing on the door."

Joe rolled over on the cushion. "So, write him a summons."

I returned to the door and waited. For some reason, Joe was suddenly taking an interest. "Well, what are you waiting for?"

Rookie or not, my patience was wearing thin as I very sarcastically responded. "Well, if I open the door right now he's going to piss on my legs." Joe just chuckled and went back to sleep, and I had my first career police action – a summons issued for urinating on the subway.

Subway Bathrooms

When I was able to get out of TPF, I was assigned to District 4 at Union Square in Lower Manhattan. It was in District 4 that I experienced one of the great moments of clarity in life. Life is filled with awakenings - those moments of awareness when total clarity sets in and you say, "Gee, I never realized...." Maybe it was that awful Christmas when you finally said, "Gee, I never realized that my parents put my presents under the tree." Perhaps it was the time your mom finally came clean about why uncle Joey was never at your birthday parties, prompting you to declare, "Gee, I never realized Uncle Joey was in jail." When I became a cop, I experienced many of these moments, but one stands out in particular, and it was the direct byproduct of being a New York City Transit Cop. It was the moment I said, "Gee, I never realized what was going on in the subway bathrooms."

As a kid growing up in Queens, my use of the subway was minimal. I walked to grammar school and high school, and by the time I went to college I was driving daily. My use of the subway consisted of three routes. From my home station of Roosevelt Avenue in Jackson Heights, a few times a year I would ride the subway to Madison Square Garden, Yankee Stadium, and Shea Stadium. That was it. If I was to ever deviate off these paths, I may as well be in a foreign country. When I think back on these rare subway experiences, I don't think I ever paused to use the bathroom in any of the stations I was in. I was not making a conscious decision to avoid the bathrooms at the time, but in retrospect, I am extremely glad that I never did use these facilities.

My first experience with subway bathrooms occurred during police academy training, when I discovered there was an actual patrol guide procedure for inspecting a bathroom. This policy instructed male officers to rap on the lady's room door with their nightstick and announce, "police inspection." I must admit that I found it odd that a police department actually had a written procedure for inspecting bathrooms.

PURPOSE: To provide procedures and guidelines for inspecting toilet facilities on the transit system
PROCEDURE MEMBER OF THE DEPARTMENT: While on routine patrol:
1. *Make thorough inspections at irregular times, at least every two hours, of all public toilets on post.*
2. *Make appropriate entries in memo book.*
3. *Inspect closed toilets and note in memo book.*
4. *Report any insanitary or other condition to the railroad clerk for notification to the proper transit authority department or comply with provisions of Accident/Irregular conditions, if situation warrants.*

NOTE: Before entering a toilet use by a member of the opposite sex member shall rap on the door and announce loudly "Police Inspection". If persons of the opposite sex are within, member shall not enter until their departure, unless informed of criminal activity therein.

Once I began patrolling subway stations I began having my "Gee, I never realized" moments. Back in the early and mid-1980s, when I did most of my subway bathroom time, the restrooms in most of the stations were open. Aside from the fact that they were filthy and smelled awful, I was oblivious to the subculture that existed in subway bathrooms.

District 4 covered the downtown Wall Street area, and I still have fond recollections of the first few times I performed solo patrol during the day tour on the Wall Street stations on the #2 line and the Lexington Avenue line. The day shift began at 7:25AM so by the time roll call was conducted and a cop traveled to post, it would be common to be calling on post from Wall Street at around 8AM. I quickly learned that whenever I arrived on post I performed a complete sweep of the entire post. Besides being proper police work, it was also an act of self-preservation. If I looked behind a stairway at 8:02AM and discovered a body, it wasn't my problem to explain - it was the problem of the cop from the prior shift. However, if I did not discover that body until 11AM, it was completely my problem, even if it really had been lying there since the prior shift. The same principle applied to the bathroom inspections. I always performed an inspection immediately after arriving on post to make sure there were no police conditions inside.

The first time I worked one of the Wall Street stations on a day shift, I strolled into the men's room at about 8:15AM. As I entered, a line of men in business suits carrying briefcases hustled past me out the door. The same thing happened during my next day tour at this station. I thought nothing of this phenomenon. I just assumed that the impending day of stock trading had these individuals nervous, causing them to make a bathroom pit stop, and once they had completed their business they were hurrying to their offices in time for the opening bell. How naïve could I have been. I mentioned my experience to a veteran officer in the district muster room and he nearly fell off the bench in laughter. When he composed himself, I was given the information for my very first "Gee, I never realized" moment on the job. I was shocked to find there was a subculture population that frequented subway men's rooms for sexual encounters. The more experience I obtained, the quicker I realized that this subculture was not bound by race, ethnicity or social status. Along with the stock brokers on Wall Street were homeless men in the men's room on the Bowery, all looking for anonymous romantic interludes.

The older I get, the more progressive I seem to get. Priorities in life are constantly changing and I have reached a point in mine where I could truly care less what type of lifestyle a person chooses to lead. I'm pretty sure, however, that if I chose to live a gay lifestyle, I wouldn't be using the subway men's room as my dating app.

There was a real wild west aspect to subway bathrooms back in the day. There was so much activity other than for their primary purpose of fulfilling a basic biological function that these areas frequently did become police problems. Predators quickly learned that open bathrooms, particularly men's rooms, supplied a large supply of potential victims - victims who would likely not look forward to reporting their victimization and necessity to explain their presence in the bathroom.

Inspecting these bathrooms daily - taking in the smell and filth and witnessing the activities taking place made a strong impression. I resolved that I would rather go in my pants than ever relieve myself in an open subway men's room. And a person would have to be especially insane to sit on a toilet seat. I learned that in the underground subculture of the subway men's room, sitting on the toilet in the stalls with no doors was code to indicate that the seated individual was open to receive visitors. How can I put this delicately? The person sitting on the toilet was very accommodating to someone stepping into the stall displaying something right before their eyes - or mouth.

One of the more disgusting stories to illustrate the subculture occurred at the Chambers Street station on a 4 x 12 tour. I was working with my partner Rick, and since the men's room at Chambers Street had a reputation for being very active, we conducted an inspection as soon as we called on post. As soon as I pushed open the door, I was nearly trampled by a throng of men scurrying out of the bathroom at the sight of a uniformed police officer. I was sure I had seen a man come jumping out of the last stall, but when I walked the length of the horrendously smelling bathroom, there was still a man sitting on the toilet in that stall. I wanted as little to do with this guy as possible so I just said, "Come on - Let's go!" as I was walking to the door. There was no movement from the stall. I held the door and again directed "I said get moving!" Still no movement. I walked back to the stall to make eye contact with this mope. "What's wrong with you? I said get out." Still silence and no movement. Despite the unsanitary environment, this guy had succeeded in getting under my skin, so now I was going to write him a summons for loitering. "Let me see some ID - what's your name?" Still no action. "You have one more chance to answer me, my friend, before you go to jail." The frightened looking man on the toilet swallowed something with a big gulp. "Sorry officer, my name is Joseph Meeks." What just happened? Use your imagination.

While on the subject of loitering, the early and mid-1980s was a bizarre time for that New York State Penal Law violation. In the early 1980s there was a section in the loitering definition that made it a violation to loiter for the purpose of engaging in deviant sex. When that section was thrown out, until the entire section could be revised, it set up a very unique situation. If I walked into a subway men's room and observed men loitering up against the wall, I could cite them for loitering. However, if these men explained that they were present to engage in sexual activity, then there was nothing I could do about it. Only in New York.

The only time I would even consider using a bathroom in the subway was when it had been locked so that only employees could use it. Let me be clear, just because a bathroom was locked for employee use did not ensure it was clean and fresh smelling. There were some locked, employee restrooms that were as bad, if not worse than the open public johns. I always considered it a bonus whenever I was working a post that included a locked, somewhat sanitary bathroom. There was nothing worse, however, then having one of these needle in a haystack, useable locked bathrooms on my post, and then screwing it up myself – example to follow.

On a very, very cold New York City winter day I was working a solo patrol post that consisted of 18th Street, 23rd Street, and 28th Street on the #1 line that runs below 7th Avenue in Manhattan. Under the adverse weather conditions, I hated this post because there was not one viable room for a break on the three stations – no crew room, signal room, or porter's room – nothing. At 18th Street, however, there was a semi-sanitary locked bathroom. To increase the value of this bathroom on such a harsh day, there was a heater partially working inside the room that made it a tolerable location. Once the morning rush hour was over and I had inspected all three stations, I returned to 18th Street to take a quick personal break and to try to get warm. The only location to accomplish this was in the locked bathroom. I keyed my way in and was pleasantly surprised to be hit by a wave of warmth being generated from the radiator. It was so comfortable that I soon removed my winter jacket and made the personal entry in my memo book to legitimize my presence therein. I then removed the folded newspaper I had stashed in my back pocket and prepared to briefly bring myself up on the current events in the world. One problem remained. It didn't really seem like a break to be standing, reading the paper. I had been standing all morning patrolling my stations, and now I wanted to sit down for a few minutes to read my paper. The choices inside this bathroom were extremely limited. I could sit on the toilet bowl, but I just found it uncouth to be sitting on the bowl for any reason other than its intended purpose. The only other possibility was to hop up on the sink to get off my feet for a few minutes. That seemed like a good idea, so I backed up to the sink, lifted myself slightly and settled my butt down on the front edge of the sink. Perfect! I read one story in the paper when – CRASH! Suddenly, I'm sitting on the floor rolling out from a steady flow of water cascading off my back. For some reason I had failed to consider that the sink would not be able to support my weight, and now the bathroom was beginning to flood. I looked around for some type of valve that would turn off the water, but there was none visible. What was I going to do now? Call on my radio that I had a flood condition at 18th Street because I was sitting on the sink reading the newspaper? I think not.

At that moment of crisis, there were two positive factors. First, this bathroom was halfway down the platform, so my entry into the room was not visible to the clerk in the token booth, and second, the bathroom was on the northbound platform. I could simply dart out of the bathroom upon the arrival of the next train and be gone to 23rd Street before anyone would know about a floor.

Furthermore, the water had not flowed yet to the extent that it was coming out to the platform from under the bathroom door. I arrived at 23rd Street and tried to forget that I had even been to 18th Street. I hung around the turnstile area for a couple of trains before proceeding to 28th Street. When I arrived at 28th Street, my radio crackled,

"Unit covering 18th Street on the #1 on the air."

"18th Street, go ahead."

"Unit covering 18th Street – there are reports of a flood on the northbound platform."

"I'm responding from 28th Street – will check and advise." I wanted to tell central that they might as well notify Transit Authority plumbers, because there was a pretty good chance the flood was real.

The greatest bathroom story I heard is likely a case of fake news. The details seem too good to be true, but nevertheless, I was told this story by several veteran officers shortly after I arrived in District 4. I'll call the cop in this story Police Officer John. The true identity of this officer meant nothing to me because I never met him. John was already retired when I heard this tale. Additionally, while I don't recall the involved station, I have a vivid memory of the specific bathroom involved because of its unique nature. Almost every usable bathroom in the system was entered in the same manner. There was a padlock on the door that was opened with a 400 key. The person entering would bring the lock inside the bathroom and secure the door with a deadbolt on the inside. This particular bathroom, however, was different. There was no padlock on this door, and a different key was inserted directly into the door handle. Once the key was turned and the door opened, it locked again automatically when it closed. The important point was that with this room there was no deadbolt to throw and someone else with a key could enter while the initial occupant was inside. This bathroom was also one of the cleaner employee restrooms in the system and it actually had doors on the two stalls.

As the story goes, Officer John took a personal break and entered the bathroom. He entered one of the stalls and sat on the toilet to complete his personal necessity. Prior to lowering his trousers and sitting, John had to remove his gun belt. Once the gun belt was off John placed it on the floor in front of his feet. The stall was small so a section of the gun belt actually protruded out from under the stall door. As John perused the newspaper and finished his business he heard the bathroom door open. While certainly not the norm, this didn't overly concern him. With this particular restroom, it was probably just another transit employee who had entered. John went back to his newspaper. As John got to the bottom of a column of newsprint, something caught his eye under the newspaper. It was his gun belt. It was moving under the stall door. It turned out that the door had never properly locked and when a homeless man passing on the platform pushed the door - it opened. The homeless man entered the bathroom and observed the gun belt sticking out partially from the stall and did what any normal person would do - he took it. John had no time to pull up his pants as he dashed out of the stall in pursuit of his gun belt. The homeless perpetrator only got about ten feet down the platform before John, pants still around his ankles, tackled him and retrieved his property. Is the story true? Probably not. But, it was quite a visual to behold if it was true.

Room with a Surprise

From my perspective in 1984, the Sony Watchman was the greatest invention of the time. For those not familiar with life during the dark ages, the Sony Watchman was the first line of pocket sized televisions that was affordable, operated via AA batteries, and actually worked – to a certain extent. During the winter of 1984, my Watchman was right up there with my service revolver, handcuffs, and memo book as must have patrol equipment. Proper deployment of the Watchman required much research. The subway environment was and still is very challenging for the use of most electronic devices, so my Watchman had to be methodically tested throughout the system to see where it would work. The big score was when optimal reception was found in a good transit room. Especially during the cold winter months, a good room on post was essential. The subway system was filled with rooms of all shapes and sizes. There were signal rooms, crew rooms, communications rooms, porter's rooms, and bathrooms, just to mention a few. Finding a room to sit and relax during meal hour was easy. Finding a sanitary room that was warm – not so easy. Finding a sanitary room that was warm and had Watchman reception – priceless.

One particular Sunday during football season, the stars seemed to be lined up perfectly for me. I was working a day tour with my partner Rick assigned to the Broadway – Nassau station. Broadway – Nassau is the downtown Manhattan subway station for the A line, but the complex we were covering also included the Fulton Street stations on the 2, 3,4,5,6 and the J lines. I had a 1PM assigned meal period that coincided with the kickoff of the Giants game. On the #2-line mezzanine was one of those rare rooms. It was a small porter's room, but it met all the criteria – a decent chair, warm, and clean. The huge bonus – perfect Watchman reception. My plan was simple. Spend my meal period in the room watching the first quarter and part of the second quarter on my Watchman. When I went off duty at the command at 4PM I would be able to watch the end of the game in the muster room. Success was on the horizon. I would get through a Sunday day tour during football season without missing the Giants game.

As 1PM approached, I was not interested in getting any food. As required, I went to the token booth and used the booth phone to call the district desk officer to put myself out to meal. I fumbled with my key ring to grab hold of my 400 key – the key that unlocked just about every lock in the system. As I approached the porter's room door, a huge sigh of relief. The padlock was in place on the door. The final obstacle to an enjoyable meal period watching the Giants was clear. Very rarely was there ever a transit porter in the room, but if there was, what was I going to do? – tell him to get out of his own room so I could watch the football game?

Key into padlock – key turned – locked removed – door opened. My dominant sense immediately became smell. The overwhelming nature of the horrendous odor seemed to push me back out of the room. The next sense to take over was sight. It did not take long to scan the tiny space for the source of the horrendous smell. Directly in front of the comfortable chair was a metal bucket.

The bucket was turned upside down, creating a very small table-like platform. The bottom of that bucket might very well have been appropriate to hold a sandwich or soda, or maybe even as the place to prop up my watchman. But alas, there was no room for my paraphrenia on the bottom of this bucket. The surface of this bucket bottom was completely covered with a fresh, steaming turd. It sat on that elevated bucket bottom like some type of art exhibit. Was this the transit porter's version of a "keep out" sign. If so, it certainly was effective. Needless to say, there was no Giants kick off for me.

In the Bag

Alcohol has long been a part of police culture. Why is that? Some will say it's part of the macho image, part of being a cop. Watch any movie portraying the life of a police officer and you are guaranteed to see a strong yet broken hero who deals with the pressures of his work with a double on the rocks. Experts on police, and many officers, say cops drink because of peer pressure and high stress levels. They get into trouble with alcohol because they feel invulnerable and, as society's helpers, are less likely to show weakness by seeking help. As mores change and technology advances, they're more likely to get caught and their colleagues less likely to risk assisting them in covering up their problems.

When I arrived in District 4 as a young, impressionable cop, the culture was alive and well. By far, the greatest pressure I faced in these fledgling days of my career was the pressure to belong – to be accepted as one of the guys. No one wanted to be ostracized – to be an outsider looking in. It was this quest for acceptance that made it so easy to get in lock step with the actions and activities of the veteran officers – including drinking – and not just off duty.

I knew many cops throughout my career who were big drinkers, but I was never personally aware of any cops who were drunk on duty. I did, however, know many veteran cops who would have a beer during their meal period. To me, it was similar to the way my dad would have a beer at dinner – no big deal. I was smart enough to realize, however, that it would be a big deal for me if I were ever caught by a supervisor drinking on duty. So, I think you are beginning to see the approaching conundrum. Left to my own devices I would never have a drink on duty, but as I previously mentioned, I desperately wanted to be accepted by all the veterans, including the drinkers. So, what would happen when I would work with a veteran who wanted to drink during our meal period? I know what you're thinking. Just let the drinker drink, but don't participate. Maybe – but it just didn't seem that easy at the time, especially when I worked with Police Office Danny.

Danny was approaching his twentieth year when I had just over a year on the job. Everybody loved Danny. He was not a macho super cop. He was just an extremely personable guy who didn't seem to have a bad word to say about anyone. He had a nice house on long island, a pretty wife, and three lovely daughters. You can see it coming, can't you. I'm about to burst the bubble by exclaiming that Danny was also a raving drunk. Sorry, I fooled you. Danny was the farthest thing from a drunk. In fact, as far as I knew, alcohol played no role in his life. For some reason, however, Danny enjoyed having a beer during his meal period. Maybe it was his longevity on the job, but he didn't seem to have any fear about doing it.

One very hot, humid summer weekday, I was working with Danny at the Chambers Street station in lower Manhattan. After an uneventful morning, it was time for our meal periods to begin. My meal was at noon and Danny's was at 1:00 PM, but I knew full well that Danny was going to sit with me in the police room during my hour. Once I had called out to meal, I did the courteous thing by asking Danny if he wanted anything while I was upstairs. Very matter-of-factly, Danny pulled a twenty dollar bill out of his pocket and said, "Get us a couple of tall boys – it's on me." For the benefit of those few souls reading this who are woefully lacking in their knowledge of beer slang, tall boys are very large cans of beer.

Chambers and Church Streets on a weekday at noon is a mass of humanity. I could feel my hands shaking when I entered the deli and removed the two cans from the refrigerator. Thankfully, the clerk must have been experienced with this type of cop purchase before because he had a brown paper bag open and at the ready when I arrived at the counter. I breathed a sigh of relief once my purchases were safely hidden inside the bag. The stress was gone. I was just like anyone else on Church street, weaving my way through the crowd with a non-descript bag in my hand – that is until the bag broke. That's right! In the midst of the Lower Manhattan lunchtime throng, the bottom of my bag gave way and the cans of beer clanked loudly on the sidewalk and began rolling away. For an instant, time seemed to stop. Whether it was real or imagined, I perceived that every eye on that sidewalk was on me, watching to see if the degenerate cop would retrieve his beer. Time quickly resumed, and I never broke stride or looked down. Like a wandering minstrel I went about my merry way, whistling a happy tune. The tall boys would remain on the curb until someone else retrieved them. When I entered the police room, I still had the empty, broken bag in my hand. Danny had a very surprised and disappointed look on his face as he asked where the beers were. I didn't say a word. I simply held up the bag and looked through the bottom like I was looking at Danny through a telescope. "Oh!" he said, before turning the page of the newspaper.

When you Gotta Go – You Gotta Go!

For most transit cops, Code 99 was akin to saying Merry Christmas or Happy Birthday. This designation was the code used for mandatory RDO (regular day off) overtime. When Code 99 was in effect, those cops like me, who were in the standard four days working, two days off schedule, switched to five days working, one day off, with the first day off being a mandatory overtime day. For most cops Code 99 was a Godsend. It provided an additional day of pay at a time and a half rate each week. For me at that time, however, Code 99 was a curse. I was single, living at home with financial concern being the last thing on my mind. All Code 99 meant to me was one day less I would be able to hang out with friends.

The Code 99 assignments were not on the regular roll calls, and they were fragmented. For example, one particular assignment required me to work 4pm x 12am. From 4pm x 6pm I was assigned to stand on the island platform of the Park Place station near City Hall in Lower Manhattan. At 6pm I would then board a northbound #2 train and ride the train to its last stop at 241st Street in the Bronx. I would then be on my one-hour meal period with the only other instructions being to return to District 4 at midnight.

As I was leaving District 4 to travel to Park Place, the day tour was returning to the command to go off duty. I ran into PO Tommy, one of my closer friends in the command. We engaged in some social small talk before I continued on to my overtime assignment. Even though Tommy was in my age range, we had polar opposite views of Code 99 overtime, considering that his household consisted of a wife and toddler. I told Tommy of my assignment to Park Place and my eventual journey to 241st Street. Tommy came up with an outstanding idea. He lived in an apartment two blocks from the 241st Street station. Tommy suggested that I have dinner at his place, hang out in his apartment until it was time to return to Manhattan, and that he would drive me back to District 4. That plan sounded great. I arrived at Park Place looking forward to the rest of the evening. At 6pm I boarded a northbound #2 train and at approximately 6:50pm I was standing on the platform at 241st Street. Also on the platform was Tommy holding his little dachshund on a leash. This was my idea of what Code 99 overtime should be. A leisurely dinner of excellent chicken parmigiana, followed by watching the Yankees on TV while enjoying a few cold brews.

      I know. I know. Everyone's alarms are sounding. Oh my God! A cop – drinking beer. First of all, I know this may be something like telling you there is no Santa Claus, but believe it or not, there have been occasions when a cop has had a drink on duty. I'm not saying it's right, but it has happened. And I'm not saying I was right, but here I was in Tommy's apartment with no other specific assignment for the rest of the night. Besides, Tommy was going to drive me back to the command, so I would not have any public contact after having a few.

      At 10:30pm I was certainly not inebriated, but I had a pleasant buzz from the beer. Tommy agreed that it was time to start making the move back to District 4. The first clue of a problem was when he could not locate his car keys. The hint of a problem quickly became an actual problem when he asked his wife for the car keys. I nearly fell off the sofa when she explained that early in the afternoon she heard a funny noise coming from the engine, and that the car was in the shop. This problem didn't seem to concern Tommy very much. He simply turned to me and said, "I guess you'll have to take the train back, buddy." This was great. With my beer buzz on, I was going to have to take the train back to the command. Before I climbed the station stairs I went into a bodega and bought three packages of mints. I kept inserting mints into my mouth until no more would fit. When I got to the platform I walked to the extreme north end of the platform. It was about 11pm and even though there are always people on the subway, regardless of the hour, I would find less people who may want to interact with me in the rear car of the train. So, there I was – standing at the end of the dark platform with no one else in sight, mouth filled with mints. Suddenly, I realized I was in big trouble. In my angst at learning that I had no car ride back to Manhattan, something had completely slipped my mind. I had not visited the bathroom during the entire evening. Now, however, it was becoming painfully clear (emphasis on painful) that I needed to go – and quick.

    I was told during my academy training that cops have to be quick decision-makers without the benefit of immediate supervision. This made sense to me. After all, I certainly didn't think it was an option to go to the payphone on the platform, call the District 4 desk officer and say, "Hey sarge, I'm at 241st Street – I've had a few beers and I need to take a leak. What should I do?" The way I saw it, my options were limited. I didn't know what time the next train would pull in, but I did know that trains ran every twenty minutes at that time of night. If I walked all the way back to the stairs and down to the mezzanine to find a bathroom on the station and missed the next train, there was no way I would make it back to the district by midnight. The last thing I needed was to have the desk officer looking for a cop who did not return at end of tour, especially when that cop had beer in him. The situation had become one of those "I have to go right now" feelings, so toughing it out all the way back to the command wouldn't work. Even if I tried that option, how humiliating would it be to lose my battle with holding it in somewhere around Times Square, providing passengers in the last car with the rare pleasure of sharing the car with the cop who pissed in his pants. In my time of distress, clarity set in, making my course of action clear. As I stood at the end of that dark platform I looked around. There was no one in sight. I unzipped and positioned myself so that the stream would flow over the edge of the platform and onto the track bed. Ahhh! The feeling of relief was immense, but it was going to take a while to complete this mission. As the flow continued there was a rumbling in the distance, but the area was still completely dark. This was the first time in my life that I had ever been on the 241st Street station, and I had not realized that the southbound trains came out of a very sharp curve as they approached the platform. As my flow continued, the distant rumbling got louder

– then, panic set in. My unzipped uniformed figure, in all its glory became illuminated by the powerful light on the front of the incoming #2 train. I wasn't done yet, so there was nothing I could do except stand there with my pants open while the motorman and a couple of passengers looking out the front door stared at the scene in disbelief. I was able to finish just as the train settled into the station and the doors opened. I slinked into the last doors in the rear car and remained there all the way back to District 4. I had learned a good lesson. What lesson? To this day, I'm not quite sure, but there must have been a lesson somewhere in that incident.

Combat Reloading

When I arrived in District 4, it was located in the Union Square subway station and covered the subway stations in Lower Manhattan. Several years prior to my arrival, the district was located in the Chambers Street station under Church Street.

The command was filled with many interesting characters. In retrospect, I suppose I could have substituted the word strange for interesting. One such character was Police Officer John. John was assigned to roll call, which meant he never went out on patrol. He was assigned to prepare the daily roll call assignments for all three platoons, so basically, he sat in the administrative area of the command typing all day. John was tall and lean, over fifty years of age with over twenty years on the job. He had an overall weather-beaten look that could likely be attributed to a familiarity with a bottle. John did not appear to be the friendliest person in the world. He never said a word to me, and frankly, I don't think I ever saw him engaged in a conversation with anyone. He just sat at his desk – typing. What stood out most about John was that he wore the department medal of honor breast bar. Since I had no dialogue with John, the details of his medal of honor would have to be supplied by others. I realize this is most likely an exaggerated urban legend, but more than one veteran officer told me this same story.

Police Officer John was still assigned to roll call at the Chambers Street command. At the end of his tour at 4pm John was in the habit of stopping in at a bar located directly adjacent to the subway entrance that led to the district. One afternoon, John was sitting in the bar nursing his drink when two males produced guns and announced a robbery. According to the story, a wild west-like shootout ensued. John produced his off-duty revolver and the bartender pulled a gun from under the bar. Both perpetrators jumped behind a table and began firing their weapons. When John ran out of ammo he darted out of the bar, with the bartender and perpetrators still engaged in a gun battle. John ran down the subway steps and into District 4. He ran past the desk officer without saying a word. He went to his desk in the administrative area and grabbed a box of ammunition from the bottom drawer. He reloaded his gun and again ran past the desk officer without saying a word. John was back up the steps, into the bar and exchanging fire again. The perpetrators ran out of ammo and surrendered. Amazingly, no one was hit. I know this story could not really have happened this way, but wouldn't it be a classic if it really did?

The Organ Grinder

The holidays were a festive time in District 4, in large part due to the district's annual Christmas party. The 1983 Christmas party was held at the Marc Ballroom located on Union Square West, just upstairs from District 4. The party had a unique concept. For $20.00 a purchaser received five tickets. In those days of a male dominated police force, the male cops attending the party were supposed to distribute the five tickets to females only. The theory being that on the night of the party, the ratio of females to males should be 5 to 1. I received my tickets about a month before the party, but as the calendar reached the week before the event, I had not handed out one ticket, and I was fast reaching the point where I was ready to give them out to anyone. I felt like someone handing out flyers as I unloaded four of the tickets to random girls during the morning rush hour at Chambers Street in Lower Manhattan. Two days before the party, however, I still had one ticket in my pocket as I sat at the bar in Kate Cassidy's a popular cop bar on Woodhaven Blvd. in Queens, and a favorite hangout for myself and many of the District 4 cops from Queens and Long Island. As I nursed my bottle of Michelob, I reached into my pants pocket to place some additional money on the bar. Instead of the cash, my hand emerged with my remaining party ticket. As fate would have it, just as I pulled out the ticket, I noticed someone enter the bar and take a seat on a stool next to me. It was Paula, still in her waitress uniform, having just completed her shift at London Lenny's, a restaurant a half block north of Kate Cassidy's. Paula was about 35 years old, with straight dirty blond hair, and a very pale complexion. She was short and thin, and although not ugly, Paula was very plain looking at best. She had been born in England and spoke with a thick British accent. Because I frequented Kate's on a regular basis and Paula would come in for a drink after finishing work, I could not help but know her. To clarify, knowing her meant that I would nod and say hello. I never really had a conversation with her or knew anything about her. On this evening, however, with the party ticket in my hand, I resolved that it would not return to my pocket.

"Evening Paula." I stated as I turned my head in her direction.

"How are you?" she said very unenthusiastically while trying to get the attention of the bartender.

I decided to make this a win-win situation for me. I took the ticket and slid it along the bar in Paula's direction. The ticket came to a stop adjacent to the twenty-dollar bill she had just placed on the bar.

I tried to sound very disinterested "My command is having a Christmas party in Manhattan Friday night and I have an extra ticket for it. If you're not doing anything, you may want to check it out."

Paula glanced at me "Maybe, thanks."

She never seemed to break out of her monotone, boring voice. I thought how she must be a load of laughs at a party, but regardless, my mission was accomplished. Even if she never removed the ticket from the bar, I didn't possess it anymore.

My partner Rick returned to his stool after a visit to the men's room. I turned to him and said, "Guess what buddy, I just got rid of my last ticket." I motioned with my head until he noticed Paula over my shoulder.

"Wow" he said with dripping sarcasm "you really hit a home run with her. She looks like the life of every party."

I sipped my beer and realized that Rick was right. By all indications, Paula was one of the most bland, unsociable people I had ever met, but at least I no longer had the ticket.

At 10:00 PM on Friday night the Marc Ballroom was hopping. A quick visual scan revealed a successful party plan as there were at least 200 females present for the 65 District 4 cops in attendance. Everyone seemed to be having a great time. The young single cops were mingling and dancing, while the older married cops were enjoying a night free of marital constraints. The music from the DJ was pulsing at a decibel level making it difficult to converse with Rick, who was seated next to me at the table along with his fiancé Letty. Letty was also a police officer in District 4, and had been in a relationship with Rick for about a year. Their romance began in a refreshingly grade school like manner by passing notes to each other in their memo book slots. For the purposes of this story it is also important to note that Rick was a little over 6-feet tall with a thick moustache, while Letty was very short, standing a hair over 5-feet.

Finally, the DJ announced a ten-minute break allowing me to momentarily hear myself think again. The party was great, but I was feeling a little bit down because I had not seen any of the females I had distributed my tickets to. I was hoping at least one of them would show up. As I conversed with Rick and Letty in a normal conversational voice, I noticed a familiar sight out of the corner of my eye. It was the distinctive black and white uniform of a London Lenny's waitress. Paula had just entered the ballroom. If I had to choose which of my ticket holders I would have preferred to make an appearance, Paula would have been last on that list, but at this point I was just happy that one of my ticket holders had arrived.

I interrupted Rick and said, "Look who's here."

Rick turned and said, "You should at least go say hello."

"You're right." I responded as I pushed back my chair.

Paula was just inside the ballroom entrance which was at least 75-feet away from me. As I walked across the dance floor I noticed that she appeared to be in conversation with several veteran cops seated at the table closest to the door. Maybe I misjudged quiet, subdued, unsociable Paula. To the contrary, she appeared to be making friends immediately. I reached a point about 20-feet away from Paula when something I heard made me stop in my tracks. Quiet, reserved Paula was addressing the veteran cops in a loud, slurred, cockeyed accent.

"Do your wives know that you're here, you scumbags?"

Oh my God, she was drunk. I watched in horror as she proceeded to the next table and pointed to Police Officer Norman, a 25-year veteran Black officer who always seemed to be in a perpetual good mood. In the next moment it was proven that even Norman could lose his good humor "Hey sambo, get me a drink."

I made an about face and a fast retreat back to my table. Paula had been far enough away that even with her loud volume, Rick had not heard her insulting tirade. I quickly briefed him on what was happening, which he found hysterical. "That's your date, buddy." he managed to get out while trying not to fall out of his seat in a fit of laughter. I could tell by the amount of people beginning to gravitate towards her direction that Paula was beginning to make an impression. I was also beginning to hear shouts of "throw her out" and "get rid of her". Then I heard the shout I was dreading "What moron gave her a ticket. Throw him out too."

It was apparent now that Paula was intent on staggering from table to table with her act, with a small crowd of onlookers, some hostile and some amused, following. My table was next in line, and I was about to take the cowardly way out and hide in the men's room, but Rick put his hand on my shoulder, forcing me back into my seat. "Oh, no buddy. Time to take your medicine." I stared down at my beer, while waiting for the drunken greeting that would likely get me tossed from the party. Paula, however, walked right past me and settled into a position standing between Rick and Letty. With her left hand on Letty's right shoulder and her right hand on rick's left shoulder, Paula looked up and announced to her following entourage, "Look what we have here. It's the organ grinder and his monkey."

Rick and Letty sat in stunned silence while I spit the beer in my mouth onto the table cloth. As if on cue, the word "monkey" had just flowed out of Paula's inebriated mouth, when the music flared up again. Putting on the Ritz, by Taco, filled the Ballroom. Paula immediately advanced to the dance floor and began performing a bizarre looking dance-march by strutting around the dance floor and waving her arms up and down. I lost sight of Paula in the increasing crowd on the dance floor, so I turned my attention back to the table to be greeted by the icy stares of Rick and Letty. I smiled weakly and shrugged. "I think she had a little too much to drink."

Eventually, Paula disappeared. I heard she performed her bizarre dance out the door and into the Manhattan night. Paula's departure was not the end of my anxiety. The other buzz going around the ballroom was the question of who had been stupid enough to invite such a despicable drunk, a mystery that I hoped would never be solved. I certainly would never tell, and I looked pathetically toward Rick in recognition of his ability to divulge my secret.

"What's it worth to you buddy? Let me think on it for a few days." he chuckled.

The following weekend found Rick and I in our usual positions at the bar of Kate Cassidy's. A little after 10:00pm Rick kicked me on the ankle and nodded to direct my attention towards the door. Paula had entered the bar. As she walked past us in the direction of an empty stool Rick turned and greeted her "Hey Paula."

She kept walking towards the empty stool, muttering "Hello" in a low tone. She then retreated into her drink as she sat at the bar, void of any conversation with others.

My sweet reserved, quiet, unsociable Paula had returned, and all was right with the world. I took a long sip of my Michelob as the jukebox sequenced to its next song. Taco's Putting on the Ritz filled the bar. I put my bottle down, scooped up my money except for a five- dollar bill tip, and was gone.

The Dirty Magazine Store

To begin this story, I need to set a scene. For over thirty years I have lived in a residential middle-class neighborhood in the New York City borough of Queens. The nearest commercial strip is on a large roadway two blocks away from my home. During my residency in the neighborhood, a 7-11 store has been very conveniently located three blocks from my home. For the first fifteen years I lived in the area, a small newspaper store was located directly adjacent to the 7-11. It was always somewhat of a mystery to me how that paper store could survive with an establishment next door that carried all the same products, and more – usually at a better price. Logic would dictate that to compete in such an environment, the small paper store would have to provide a product not available at the 7-11. Let's see – newspapers? No good. 7-11 carries all the papers. Beer and soda? Nope. 7-11 has a better selection. Candy and snacks? 7-11 wins there too. There must be some product to separate the small newspaper store from 7-11. There was – pornographic magazines.

I was no connoisseur of pornographic magazines, but I would bet the ranch that this small store had one of the largest collections of porno magazines in the city. How would I have the data to form such an opinion? Product placement! These magazines were not hidden in some back room or shielded by a partition. When a customer walked through the entrance door, he/she was staring at a wall of magazines that ran from the floor to the ceiling. The magazines were such a visible part of the store that for the entire time the store was open my family never referred to the establishment as the newspaper store, paper store, or newsstand. In my household it was universally called the dirty magazine store.

I didn't browse or buy the dirty magazines, but I also possessed no sense of moral outrage preventing me from patronizing the dirty magazine store. In fact, I found it interesting to recognize the informal protocols that seemed to be in place for the purchase of dirty magazines. A customer would get the clerk's attention and quickly pass the selected magazine(s) to the clerk at the side of the counter. The customer would then proceed to the counter where purchases were processed, and his purchase would be waiting in a plain brown bag.

Ok, I know. Why am I droning on about pornographic magazines? Well, as I mentioned, I had to set a scene, and now that scene is set.

In 1967, the Presidents Commission on Law Enforcement and Administration of Justice determined that there was a greater need for the proper training of police officers. It recommended no fewer than 400 hours of instruction and a 12- to 18-month probationary period. It also recommended no fewer than 8 weeks of field training and college education for different levels of police officers. When I graduated the police academy in 1982 cops had to attend one full day of in-service training each year as well as pass a firearms qualification annually. It was sometime during the winter of 1983 that I was directed to complete the annual firearms qualification. I know you are probably cringing, but I have to set one more scene.

Two days before the scheduled firearms qualification a blizzard struck New York City. The snow began in the late afternoon and continued through the night and into the next day. When it was over, more than two feet of snow covered the city. I had been on a regular day off when the snow began. In fact, I was enjoying the winter afternoon with a group of friends inside Kate Cassidy's Pub in the Rego Park section of Queens. Afternoon transitioned to evening and the snowed piled deeper and deeper. The weather had no effect on the atmosphere inside the pub. The good times continued to roll late into the evening. This was my first RDO, so I was also off duty the next day. Let it snow! Sometime around midnight it occurred to me that it may be time to head home. Surprise, surprise. My car was buried and the roads were impassable. One of my friends in the pub lived in an apartment across the street, so I spent the night on his sofa. By 11AM the next morning the snow had stopped, but traffic was still non-existent. There was no way I was going to get my car out, and even if I did, there was nowhere to go. If I was going to get home, I was going to have to walk four miles. The walk itself was not a tremendous effort for a 26-year-old in good physical condition, but factor in the two feet of snow that still covered most of the roads and sidewalks and you had a very different challenge. I made it home as the sun was setting. I ate supper and went to bed. I had to get up extra early to take public transportation to the firearms qualification. Second scene set. I promise – no more scene setting.

The Transit Police firearms range was in the basement of a transit police facility at 300 Gold Street in downtown Brooklyn. These were the days before any department was even thinking about using semi-automatic pistols. Everyone used revolvers. In my case I had a Smith & Wesson Model 10, 4-inch service revolver and a 2-inch Smith & Wesson Chief as an off-duty weapon. I completed the qualifying course of fire without a problem. For the last phase of the qualification, the instructor running the line directed the shooters to holster their weapons and draw their off-duty weapons. All that remained was to fire five rounds from my Chief. I always carried my off-duty weapon in an ankle holster, so, after holstering my service revolver I reached down to my left ankle and drew my Chief. The orders came from the range master,

"Ready on the right? Ready on the left? Ready on the firing line?"

At the buzzer I began the slow steady trigger pull I had been taught during recruit training. Nothing happened. I pulled a little harder on the trigger. Still nothing. Finally, with no regard for trigger control I yanked as hard as I could on the trigger, but it didn't budge. As was drilled into my head during firearms training, my non-shooting hand shot up to alert an instructor of a problem. Firearms instructor Police Officer L. appeared at my point and took possession of my Chief. After a few seconds of manipulation, he chuckled. "What the hell did you do? It's rusted shut."

I was embarrassed because I instantly knew exactly what had happened. During my four- mile sojourn through the two feet of snow, guess where my Chief was? You guessed it – on my left ankle, getting more and more saturated with each step. I can classify it as pure stupidity that it never occurred to me when I got home that I should at least open up the gun and dry it off. PO L. was being a complete gentleman about the situation – more so than I could have hoped for. He quietly told me not to worry and that it was no big deal. He took my gun back to their armory and fifteen minutes later I had my gun back in perfect condition. A happy ending to the story, right. Not so fast. I had no sooner snapped the Chief into the ankle holster when I heard a bellow,

"Officer Bryan, report to the supervisor's office."

Sergeant K. was the firearms unit supervisor. I don't know what, if any military background the sergeant possessed, but he certainly carried himself like a gung-ho marine. From his high and tight haircut, to his broad shoulders and thin waist, to his starched uniforms and highly shined shoes, Sgt. K. really looked the part. He also sounded the part too, as he proceeded to verbally go up one side of me and down the other in lambasting my stupidity in failing to take proper care of my firearm. The good sergeant finished the session by formally writing me up for failing to take care of my weapon. Before you conclude that this is just a sour grapes rant on my part, let me make something perfectly clear. I was one hundred percent wrong. What if something had happened on my way to the range that day where I needed to use my weapon? I took full responsibility for my malfeasance. I just wish he could have handled it a little differently, but he was the sergeant, and was perfectly within his rights to write me up and humiliate me.

Fast forward a couple of years, and I am now living in my current residence. I entered the dirty magazine store to get some soda and to make some copies. These were the days before home computers and printers and the dirty magazine store had a five-cents per copy machine in the back. I made my copies and grabbed my soda out to the refrigerator. When I went to the counter to pay, the customer who had been browsing the porno wall was following the usual protocol in slipping a handful of magazines to the clerk at the side of the counter. I arrived at the counter to pay at the same time the porno customer arrived. Wait a minute, the porno customer was Sgt. K. My smile could not have gotten wider as I said "Hey sarge, how are you doing?"

His eyes widened and his face turned red. He made a few stuttering sounds but no audible words came out. I realized how evil I was being, but I had no intention of letting him off the hook. "I didn't know you lived around here, sarge. They have a lot of nice things in here for such a small store, don't they?"

Sgt. K. would not make eye contact, and his face was turning a deeper shade of red. The clerk announced "Next!" Sgt. K. continued to avoid eye contact, but said "Go ahead."

I still wasn't done with the torture, however. "No, no – go ahead, sarge. I insist." I very courteously waved my arm in a sweeping motion as a guide for the sergeant to the counter. I must say I thoroughly enjoyed watching every moment of the red-faced sergeant paying and accepting his plain brown bag. Sgt. K. did not acknowledge me as he began to depart with his bag, but I was certainly not going to be discourteous.

"Take care, sarge. Maybe I'll see you again."

He never looked back.

Bumpy

Another interesting character in District 4 was Police Officer Bumpy. Obviously, Bumpy wasn't his real name, but it took only one time working with him to understand how he received the moniker. When I arrived in District 4 Bumpy had over sixteen years on the job. He was tall and heavyset, and during my one experience working with him I found out he lived in the same Queens neighborhood as I did. The most enduring memory of my day working with Bumpy, however, was the appropriate nature of the nickname.

We were working the West 4th Street Station in Greenwich Village. The station was long – running along 6th Avenue from West 3rd Street to West 8th Street. Whether we were patrolling on the upper or lower platforms, the mezzanine, or the street, we would be walking together as we patrolled five blocks back and forth. Why did the length and direction of walk matter? It shouldn't, but this is where Bumpy comes in. For some reason, he couldn't walk more than ten steps without veering into me. He was a very big guy, and it would quickly become unsettling to constantly get "bumped" into as we patrolled. I thought he was being a wise ass, but it quickly became apparent that his nickname was well earned. For whatever reason, the man was constantly angling towards me as he walked, so every few feet, Bumpy bumped me. I don't know if his center of gravity was off, maybe one leg was shorter than the other. Who knows? I was just thankful I never worked with him again. If I wanted to experience bumper cars I could go to an amusement park.

Speaking of cars, I had one other interesting (or strange) experience with Bumpy. I previously mentioned that Bumpy lived in my Queens neighborhood, but I didn't say how I discovered this fact. For years, one of the commercial cornerstones of the neighborhood was a shopping center. The center occupied one square block with the stores in an L-shape adjacent to a very large parking lot. I lived a few blocks from the shopping center, and with the convenience of a supermarket, drug store, dry cleaners, and newsstand, I was in the shopping center several times a week. The frequency of my visits allowed me to observe a cottage industry spring up in the parking lot. It began with one or two guys, but within a few months there was more than a dozen industrious entrepreneurs roaming the parking lot asking drivers if they would like the dents removed from their cars. I was the target audience for these businessmen because my car had several small dents in various areas. I never availed myself of these services, but the pitch was usually the same. The guy would have a rubber hammer and some tool to pull the dent out, and he would quickly approach with "Get rid of your dents for fifty bucks?" When I declined, he was quickly gone to his next potential customer. Receiving this pitch became common, so there was no surprise when I parked to drop off uniforms at the dry cleaners, and as soon as I stepped out of my car I heard the familiar, "Get rid of your dents for fifty bucks?" What was different on this occasion was who was making the offer. Standing before me with his rubber hammer and dent-pulling tool was Bumpy. I was expecting some acknowledgement or at least the punch line to the joke, but it quickly became apparent that this was Bumpy's side job, and it was just as apparent that Bumpy had no idea that I was a cop from his own command. I smiled and shook my head, and like he was shot out of a cannon, Bumpy was off to find his next potential customer. I never saw him move so fast on patrol, which was probably a blessing. If Bumpy had bumped me at the speed he was moving in the parking lot, I would have ended up on the tracks.

Ring Around the Rosie (or the Booth)

When I arrived in District 4 in 1982 female cops had ceased being a novelty, but they certainly were not plentiful on the job. In a command with a little over a hundred cops, there may have been ten females at that time. As my career progressed I would learn that there was no real difference in the policing abilities of the two sexes. I worked with many great male and female cops, and I also knew horrible cops that came in both sexes. After I had been in District 4 for about six months, I began noticing an interesting phenomenon. The command was almost an even split between single and dual patrol posts. So, for an average tour, half the cops turning out would be teamed with a partner and the other half would be patrolling solo. For the most part, these roll call assignments were fairly distributed, but one day it occurred to me that I had never noticed any of the females assigned to solo patrol.

One day, during a day tour, I was working with George, a fifteen-year veteran who had spent most of his career in the command. I informed George of my observation that the females never worked alone and he just laughed. George then proceeded to provide the answer to my question. First, a disclaimer moment. This story was second hand. I had no direct knowledge of its veracity, but I did end up hearing the same story from several other sources.

George said that it was the commanding officer's policy not to have any of the females work alone because of an incident that occurred about a year earlier. George stated that like all the females in the command at that time, Felicia had less than a year on the job. On a midnight shift, Felicia was assigned to work alone on three stations on the Lexington Avenue line – 23rd Street, 28th Street, and 33rd Street. At all of these stations, there was no mezzanine level, so the token booth was located at platform level, just outside the turnstiles. The southbound side of 33rd Street had the best set up for a cop who was trying to write "fare-beat" summonses. The cop could stand on the platform next to the slam gate without being visible to anyone outside the turnstiles. If a person walked through the gate without paying the fare, they were literally two steps from the waiting cop before they would even realize the cop was there.

On this particular midnight shift at around 3AM, Felicia decided to see if she could write a few summonses at 33rd Street. She stood up against the wall on the southbound platform at 33rd Street and waited. It only took a couple of minutes for a large, middle age male to come strolling through the gate. Felicia performed the correct tactical move by taking the male out to the token booth area to write the summons. It was never a good idea to write a summons on the platform, where the platform edge was always in close proximity. As Felicia progressed with the interaction, the male was becoming increasingly belligerent. Since it was 3AM on a weekday during the winter, there was no one else in the area except the clerk inside the token booth. At some point Felecia realized she had a problem, so she stepped back and drew her nightstick. The moment the stick cleared the holder, the male pounced. Leaping forward and grabbing the stick out of Felicia's grasp.

The fight-or-flight response, also known as the acute stress response, refers to a physiological reaction that occurs in the presence of something that is terrifying, either mentally or physically. The response is triggered by the release of hormones that prepare your body to either stay and deal with a threat or to run away to safety. The term 'fight-or-flight' represents the choices that our ancient ancestors had when faced with a danger in their environment. They could either fight or flee. In either case, the physiological and psychological response to stress prepares the body to react to the danger.

In Felicia's case, the choice was swift and certain – she ran. The male, whose intoxicated state likely contributed to his actions, also decided on a quick course of action – he pursued. Felicia ran, with the male in hot pursuit. She did not run upstairs or onto the platform. Instead, she began circling the token booth. The clerk inside the booth watched in amazement as the drunk male waving the nightstick chased the fleeing uniform police officer. After several laps around the booth the clerk picked up his booth phone and called for police assistance. Still, the chase continued. Who knew how long it would take for the cavalry to arrive. It what sounded eerily familiar to a Three Stooges or Laurel and Hardy Movie scene, the clerk grabbed a baseball bat he kept stashed away in the booth. He then opened the booth door, waited until Felicia had run past, and then smashed the drunk on his head with the bat. Pursuit terminated.

George said that after the Captain was given the details of the incident, he decided that while he was commanding officer of the district, there would never be another time a uniform cop was being chased round and round a token booth by a drunk. His solution – never let any of the female cops work alone again.

Chief Stories

When I was appointed to the Transit Police Department, and was assigned to District 4, Chief James was the chief of the department. Here are two stories about the chief that were circulating District 4 when I arrived.

At the time I came on the job, there were many issues between the cops and the department administration. One of the more pressing concerns was the issue of two-man patrol. Due to the immense size of many of the Manhattan subway stations, there were a considerable amount of dual patrol posts in Midtown and Downtown Manhattan. The basic transit assignment, however, was solo patrol. Add in the fact that radio communications in the subway was sporadic at best, and the one-man patrol posts could be very dangerous.

The Transit Patrolman's Benevolent Association pressed hard for universal two-man patrol, but Chief James held out firmly against it. One day just before I came on the job, the union held a rally outside Transit Police headquarters at 370 Jay Street in downtown Brooklyn. Hundreds of cops massed on the street below the chief's office to march, chant and wave signs. Most of the signs were produced by the union and were not terribly controversial. Police Officer Steve, a cop from District 4 was not going to depend on his union. He showed up at the rally with his own large, homemade sign. Steve's sign, which he proudly held up in the direction of the chief's office window read "CHIEF JAMES – PLEASE JUMP."

Steve's sign easily would have taken the prize for most popular, as evidenced by the hundreds of cops chanting JUMP – JUMP- JUMP as Steve pumped the sign up and down in his hands, keeping time to the chant.

Nothing really changed, but I believe the chief added a couple of new dual patrol posts in the city, but a lot of bad will had been established between the chief and the rank and file cops. To ease the tension, Chief James embarked on a morale building goodwill tour where he began addressing roll calls in all the Transit Police districts throughout the city. When he got to District 4, the goodwill didn't last long. The chief addressed a 4 x 12 roll call that Police Officer Steve just happened to be a part of. After a very few opening remarks regarding how everyone needs to work together as a team, the Chief paused and seemed to be focusing on something or someone in the rows of assembled cops. Very quickly the chief's focal point became clear. "You!" He pointed to the third row at Officer Steve. "You held that sign telling me to jump. I won't forget that!"

So much for the spread of goodwill. Right after that inspiring roll call message, Police Officer Steve went out sick due to stress. It was my understanding that he never came back and left the job with a medical disability pension.

Police Officer Frank worked regularly with Steve, and he never forgot how the Chief's threat chased his partner off the job. About a year after the roll call morale boost, Frank was on post and came upon some religious sect handing out literature on the station.

For reasons known only to Frank, he happened to have Chief James home address on him, so he very happily filled out the cult's questionnaire, requesting that additional information regarding the group should be sent to Chief James at his home address. When Chief James began getting mailings and phone calls from the group at his home in Brooklyn, he assigned detectives from the Transit Police Special Investigation Unit to work the case. They very quickly fingered Frank as the culprit, and he confessed and took a 30-day suspension rather than risk being terminated. It just goes to show what good detective work can do in instances of such an important case.

On to the Academy

I thoroughly enjoyed my two years as a recruit police academy instructor. Being shy and reserved by nature, I had tremendous reservations about my ability to get up in front of a classroom and speak. Surprisingly, I thrived in the public speaking environment. Since my first experience in the police academy a significant segment of my life has been involved in some form of public speaking. In the police department I instructed several in-service and specialized training programs, as well as facilitating methods of instruction courses, where I taught cops how to be instructors. Outside the job I am still an adjunct college professor and I teach the insurance reduction defensive driving classroom course. In retrospect, beginning my public speaking experience with recruit police officers was probably a big advantage. The recruits were the classic captive audience. They had to sit quietly and appear attentive, regardless of the mistakes I may have made.

I never understood the attitude that some of my fellow instructors possessed. As a Transit Cop, detailed to the NYPD Police Academy, this was the greatest assignment I could possibly obtain. Think about it, one day I am riding northbound/southbound, inhaling subway steel dust, and the next day I am molding young recruit minds. The biggest benefit to being an academy instructor by far, however, was the work schedule. For the two years I was assigned to the academy, operations were run in two squads. This meant that classes were conducted Monday through Friday with weekends off. The squads flip flopped, so one week I would work day tours with the following week being 4 x 12 shifts. I was assigned to the police science department. Instructors were assigned two recruit companies, with academic classes being 90-minutes in duration. So, on an average day, an instructor spent three hours in the classroom. The remainder of the time was for the instructor to do as he or she pleased. If the instructor was prepared for class, the down time could be used working out with weights, playing basketball or racquetball in the gym, or jogging down by the East River. No one seemed to care where you were as long as you were in the classroom on schedule. How could anyone have a negative attitude with this type of assignment?

One of my direct supervisor's in the police science department was sergeant Sean. Like me, Sean was detailed to the NYPD Police Academy from the Transit Police. Sean was a great guy and I loved working for him. The issue with Sean was that he fancied himself something of an intellectual giant, when the reality was that Sean's mouth was regularly several steps ahead of his brain. In other words, it was common for Sean to speak without fully weighing the ramification of his words. A case in point was the stress exercise.

Police work has been described as 90% boredom with the remaining 10% being sudden bursts of stress and fear. The recruit curriculum was filled with role plays to prepare recruits to handle these stressful, dangerous situations. But they were simulations, and no matter how realistic they were scripted, they could never stimulate the actual physiological responses that would occur during one of these stressful situations. As soon as a person feels fear, the amygdala (a small almond-shaped organ in the center of the brain) sends signals to the autonomic nervous system (ANS), which then has a wide range of effects. The ANS kicks in, and suddenly, the heart rate increases, the blood pressure goes up, the breathing gets quicker, and stress hormones such as adrenaline and cortisol are released. The blood flows away from the heart and out towards the extremities, preparing the arms and legs for action. The ability to think and reason decreases as time goes on, so thinking about the next best move in a crisis can be a hard thing to do. A roleplay regarding the response to a man with a gun can be scripted with an amazing amount of detail, but at the end of the day, the recruit in the roleplay ultimately is aware that it is a simulation and does not experience the aforementioned physiological responses. So, the question became – can anything be done during academy training to stimulate the actual physiological responses to fear. The simple answer – you have to scare the recruits. But how do you do it in a safe, controlled environment. Answer – the stress exercise. During the first week of training, all the recruits were given a drug test. Once the results of these tests were in, and it was confirmed that there were no failures, the stress exercise could begin.

   The squad sergeants from the three academic disciplines – police science, social science, and law, were required to enter a classroom in the middle of an instruction period. In their hands, the sergeants carried a folder that had boldly written on it "DRUG TEST FAILURES." The sergeant would stand in the front of the room making it very easy for the class to see the writing on the folder. He would then somberly read out five pre-selected names from the recruit company and instruct them to quickly gather all their belongings and come with him out of the room. After the sergeant and his group departed, the fear in the room was palpable. The most intense fear was reserved for the five who had been removed from the class and told they had failed the drug test, and that their careers were over before they began.

On this day that Sergeant Sean broke into my classroom displaying his folder, it was during my second recruit training class, so I had been through this stress exercise once before. Sean dramatically called the names from the folder to the front of the room and departed with his devastated crew. I was left with a classroom now in a state of shock. After a few minutes I revealed the nature of the exercise to the class, and I anticipated the return of the failing five. The class period ended, however, without the return of the five recruits. I returned to the police science office to find out what had happened. I found Sean sitting in his office working furiously on paperwork.

I stuck my head in and asked, "Everything go alright with the exercise?"
The look on Sean's face indicated a complete lack of recognition. "The stress exercise," I clarified.

"Oh shit!" Sean blurted as he pushed past me and out of the police science office.

It seemed that while Sean was in the hall stimulating stress from the five recruits, a recruit from a different company ran up to him and reported that a different recruit had fallen in the cafeteria and was bleeding heavily from the head. Sean ran to the location of the injured recruit while leaving the five standing in the hall with all their gear, believing they had been terminated. Sean became completely immersed in the injured recruit and the ensuing paperwork. Until I stuck my head in his office, he had completely forgotten about the five recruits he had left hanging in the hall. Now Sean was experiencing the physiological response to fear. The five recruits were gone. And why not. A sergeant had just informed them they had failed a drug test and were fired. When the sergeant ran off, what were they supposed to do? They went home. The lieutenant chairman of the police science was also undergoing physiological changes. His responses, however, were not limited to fear. The lieutenant had an awful lot of anger coming through. Anger directed at Sergeant Sean. The lieutenant did not care who heard him lashing out at Sean. "How could you be so stupid!" – "What if they jump in front of a train?" The lieutenant's physiology did not return to normal until all five recruits had been contacted. What about Sean? That was the great thing about him. The next day he was back to normal – ego fully intact. In his mind, he had administered the ultimate stress exercise.

A Day in the Country

I worked as a patrol cop in District 4 for five years. I spent the next two years detailed as an instructor at the NYPD Police Academy. I left the academy upon my promotion to sergeant and was assigned back to District 4. At first, I was happy to be returning to my familiar stomping ground. Shortly after arriving, however, there were times when working as a supervisor became a bit uncomfortable. I had many close friends in the command who were still present when I returned as a sergeant. For most of these friends my rank of sergeant was a non-issue, but every now and then I would run into issues with those friends who were prone to running scams.

Police Officers Doug and Howie were good guys, but they were always on the prowl for a good scam. They were both part of my academy class, and during our recruit training Howie got jammed up when without invitation, he was caught trying to climb through the bedroom window of a female recruit. That sure sounded an awful lot like burglary, trespass, or any number of illegal offenses, but somehow Howie survived. Doug was a charter member of a group of cops known as District 4's Rat Pack. The Rat Pack consisted of four or five cops out of my academy class who seemed to always be involved in some type of shenanigans. A case in point was the day a sergeant or lieutenant on a day tour made the terrible mistake of assigning four members of the Rat pack, including Doug, to a plainclothes detail. Mike K. and Mike J. were working as one team, while Doug was paired with Joey. Once the second platoon was turned out, where did our cadre of plainclothes officers go? Did they go to the Second Avenue station to stake out a robbery pattern? Did they proceed to the Bowery to address the rash of bag snatches that had occurred on the station over the past two months? Maybe they went up to Grand Central to work pickpockets during the morning rush hour.

By 9AM they were all in Doug's car driving across the George Washington Bridge. This was much too nice a day to spend fighting crime in the subway. This was a day perfect for a trip to the country. The destination was somewhere in the Poconos, but the plan to commune with nature began to unravel when Doug's car began to overheat on Route 80.   Doug pulled to the side of the highway to investigate the problem. He opened the radiator cap to a still very hot radiator and got seriously burned all over his face. Needless to say, the boys were in some deep shit. Obviously, they couldn't get him medical attention right away as that might be a hard one to explain to the desk officer. So, they quickly decided to get a motel room and have Doug soak his steam ravaged body in the bathtub. Joey stayed with Doug while the Mikes got the car going and made it back to the command. There, they were able to sign everyone back for end of tour and then return to the motel in New Jersey to continued nursing Doug back to health. Somehow, no one of any importance ever found out about this stunt.

The Unreachable Star

One of the huge benefits of being part of the civil service system was the job security. Once off probation, the analogy often used was that a cop would have to shoot the Chief to get fired. While there was a degree of truth associated with that analogy, if you worked hard enough at it, eventually, you could get fired, but reaching the threshold of termination was like the old song – the unreachable star.

As crazy as the Rat Pack's antics could be, they were basically likeable guys, and they stayed within the parameters of at least semi-sane behavior. Sometimes, however, there are actions taken where all you can do is shake your head and ask – why? Such was the case with Police Officer Kevin.

One night, during a 4x12 tour, PO Kevin was working a solo patrol post in District 4. I guess Kevin decided he had more pressing issues besides patrol, so he drove his own car home to spend the rest of the night lounging in his residence. Bear in mind, his residence was not within the confines of District 4. It wasn't even in Manhattan – his home was in Brooklyn.

Fate can be a funny thing. At some point during his leisurely evening at home, Kevin happened to look out his apartment window and sees two knuckleheads breaking into his car. He ran downstairs just in time to see his taillights fading in the distance.

There are times when you have to regroup, cut your losses and move on. This was likely one of those times. Running out of your home just in time to see two mopes driving away in your car is not a pleasant picture, but you have to assess the entire situation. At the time his vehicle was on its way to parts unknown, PO Kevin was supposed to be patrolling a post in Manhattan. I'm not sure what the best action would have been to try to salvage the situation. Perhaps waiting until after midnight, and then reporting the car stolen to make it look like he discovered it missing when he got home after work. That certainly wasn't honest or ethical, but it might have worked. Even though I wasn't sure what the best action to take was, I had a very good idea of what the absolute worst thing to do would be. That worst action would be pursuing the car thieves. No one in their right mind would consider a pursuit. What good could come of it when he was supposed to be on patrol in a different borough. Well, what do you think PO Kevin decided to do? That's right – an immediate pursuit. But how is he pursuing when his vehicle is the subject of his chase? This is where Kevin enters into the hall of fame of idiotic decisions. As Kevin is watching his car disappear into the night, a New York City bus begins to pass by. Before he was a cop, Kevin was a bus driver. You can see what's about to happen, can't you? That's right. Kevin commandeers the bus and takes off in pursuit of his car. This ridiculous scene gets even better. How could it, you ask? Well, he actually caught the perpetrators and ended up shooting them.

    When the smoke cleared, PO Kevin had reached that nearly unreachable star, and was fired, but amazingly, that's not the end of the story. He fought his termination and incredibly got his job back. On top of that, he made sergeant! Sadly, his winning streak ended there. I found out years later that Sgt. Kevin got jammed up again and managed to reach the unreachable star for a second time. This time, the trip out the door was permanent.

Can't We All Just Get Along

Remember the story about the female being chased around the token booth? Could there be anything worse that a cop in uniform being chased by a drunk? Actually, there was. How about two uniformed cops in a fistfight on patrol.

Police Officer Tommy was a great guy. He graduated from the same academy class as I did, and you could not find a more solid, loyal guy than Tom. Well, nobody's perfect, and Tom's big imperfection was a hair trigger temper. He could be set off very easily by the public, or other cops.

Police Officer Peter was gay. I hate playing identity politics, but this was Peter's style. I could care less about a cop's sexual orientation. The only important identity was that of a good cop. Peter, however, was way ahead of the times. In an era when very few cops were openly gay, Peter was "in your face" with his sexuality. It was as if he would introduce himself as – "I'm Peter and I'm gay – want to make something of it?"

In retrospect, it may not have been a good idea to have Tom and Peter working together during the afternoon rush hour at the 59th Street and Lexington Avenue station in Midtown Manhattan. To this day, I still don't know the cause, but I remember the event like it was yesterday. I was a new sergeant back in my old stomping ground of District 4. I was a patrol supervisor on a 4x12 shift, and at 7PM I returned to the command with my driver for our meal period. I stopped off at the desk to talk with Sergeant Richie. While we were talking, a phone call was picked up by the assistant desk officer. He interrupted our conversation to tell Richie that the token booth clerk from 59th street wanted to speak with him. There was a degree of stress in the ADO's voice that made me decide to stay and see what the call was about. I could only hear Richie's side of the conversation, which consisted of a series of "What?" and "You're kidding." When he hung up, Richie had a glazed look in his eyes. I asked what had happened, but he raised his index finger to stop my inquiry while he grabbed a portable radio with his other hand. The sergeant in the sector covering 59th Street was on the road, and during that era, the sergeant's car was referred to as "King" over the radio. Richie's transmission went something like this.

"4-king on the air."

"4-king, go ahead."

"4-king, proceed to 59th Street forthwith, southbound plat. – see the railroad clerk – forthwith."

"4-king 10-4 – two minutes out."

Two times using forthwith – calling direct and not going through the communications unit. What the heck was going on? Richie shook his head and explained. The clerk in the booth said the two uniform cops on the station were in a fight – with each other.

He told Richie that they were punching and wrestling while a crowd of subway riders gathered around to watch the cops fight.

That incident ended about as well as it could under the circumstances. Neither Tommy or Peter was arrested, and unlike today, there were no photos or videos of the uniform cops rolling around on the platform. They were both written up formally for conduct unbecoming a police officer and received a couple of days suspension, but all in all, they both got off very cheaply. To this day, I am still not certain of what caused the brawl.

Next Stop - Siberia

I was working as the patrol supervisor in the lower sector on a 4 x 12 tour, with Police Officer Mike as my driver. At 8:00pm Mike parked the RMP at Union Square and we descended into District 4 for our meal period.

As I passed the desk, I heard a very gruff, "Hey Bryan, don't get comfortable, I got something for you."

It was the district desk officer, good old personable Lt. B., affectionately known as "Screwy Louie." This was the same jerk who a sent me to be evaluated for an alcohol problem a few years earlier (Shameless promotion – for that sordid tale, you have to read *Dark Knights*).

"I'm on meal, Lou."

Before I could finish my thought, he cut me off. "Your meal has to wait. I need you to do something now."

I stood in front of the desk waiting for instructions. Lt. B. pointed to a man sitting on the bench just inside the district door. Leaning forward on the bench was a very uncomfortable looking white male who appeared to be about 40 years of age. He was tall and husky with short brown hair and had the look of someone who was no stranger to strenuous labor. He was dressed casually, but very neatly in a brown, short sleeve collared shirt, tan slacks and black dress shoes.

"Yes?" I replied to Lt. B. in an attempt to communicate that I was not a mind reader.

Lt. B. impatiently handed a piece of paper to me and dismissively added "Get him back to his ship." The paper had "Pier 6 - Brooklyn" scribbled in pen on it, so I approached the man to obtain some additional information.

"How are you sir? Is this where you need to go?" I said while displaying the paper to him. The man began a frantic sounding babble that I believed to be in the Russian language. I held up my outstretched right hand in the universal sign for stop and returned to the district desk.

"He speaks Russian." I commented to Lt. B. who was now hard at work flipping through various menus. I gathered that he had no intention of forfeiting his meal period.

"I'm well aware that he speaks Russian," he stated in an annoyed tone.

"Well, don't you think we should find an interpreter?" I countered.

"Look sergeant, I don't have an interpreter and I don't speak Russian, do you?"

I just stood silently while the lieutenant continued, "Just take him back to his ship. Now get out of here!"

I motioned for the man to follow me, and several minutes later, Mike was driving towards the Brooklyn Bridge. With a language like Spanish, even if you don't speak the language, you can still get an idea of what is being said because many of the words are similar in formation. Not with Russian, however. This man was going on and on in the back seat and I had no clue of what he was talking about. The one emotion that I did pick up on was that he appeared to be nervous.

We got to Pier 6 on the Brooklyn side of the river and entered through the vehicle gate. The scene was similar to an old mystery movie – dark and quiet, with a dimly lit ship moored in the distance. As the RMP drew closer to the ship I could see the hammer and sickle flag of the Soviet Union flying from the bow. Our passenger was becoming more and more frantic in the back seat as he figured out that we were returning him to the ship. I was really uncomfortable with what we were about to do, and I wanted to give it one more try with Lt. B. I directed Mike to drive back to the street and find a pay phone. I called the District 4 desk, and my conversation with Lt. B. went something like this:

"Lieutenant, I think we should reconsider returning this guy to his ship."

"What are you talking about?"

"I think this guy may be trying to defect."

Now Lt. B. began to scream. "DEFECT! DEFECT! Who said anything about defecting. I don't want to hear that word again. If you don't get him on that ship, you better be on it – Understand, sergeant!"

"Understood."

I know this is a horrible analogy, but when we returned to the dock, and I let this man with fear in his eyes out of the RMP, I felt like a cruel pet owner who let a scared little puppy out on the side of a highway – nothing good was going to happen.

When I walked into the district, Lt. B. was quick to question me. "You got that guy on his ship, didn't you?"

"I sure did, Lou. He's probably on his way to Siberia as we speak."

"Good," Lt. B. said as he took his next bite of Chinese food.

The Chief is a Bully

When I attended the instructor's course at the NYPD Police Academy, the lead instructor said that once you become an instructor, training gets in your blood. He compared the Police Academy to a giant rubber band. The instructor said that academy personnel may leave their training assignments for promotions or other assignments, but that at some point the rubber band always eventually pulls them back to the academy.

Once I had been a patrol sergeant in District 4 for several months I was looking to strap into that rubber band and let it shoot me back to the Police Academy. It took about a year, but finally the rubber band did its job. The only problem was that there must have been too much tension on the band, because I was shot right past the NYPD Police Academy and instead landed in the Transit Police Academy at 300 Gold Street in Brooklyn. To make matters worse I was assigned as the administrative sergeant for the academy. I really wasn't looking forward to this administrative position and I told the commanding officer as much. The C.O. explained that if I put my heart into the administrative sergeant job, as soon as a sergeant vacancy occurred at the NYPD Police Academy, he would transfer me. That seemed fair enough. To be frank, I do not look back fondly at my two-year stint as the administrative sergeant. In my prior assignment as an instructor, academy work had involved classroom instruction and curriculum development, both of which I enjoyed. There were sergeants at the NYPD Police Academy who were still in the classroom, but I realized that the academy role as a sergeant was going to be different – I just didn't realize how different.

Shortly after my assignment as the administrative sergeant, there was a major shakeup in the Transit Police Department. A new, high profile department chief from Boston was hired, and he immediately began re-energizing a department whose identity for years had been the role of step child of the massive NYPD. The Chief was not content to follow the lead of the NYPD, but instead took the lead in many areas. The Transit Police transitioned to 9mm semi-automatic pistols long before the NYPD considered the change. The only difference in the NYPD and Transit Police uniforms was the patch worn. The new chief, however, began to institute uniform changes that the NYPD did not have, such as the authorization of a commando sweater as a uniform item. It was obvious that the new chief was moving quickly, and part of his process of change was the seemingly never-ending schedule of meetings and conferences with his command staff and representatives from other police departments around the country and the world.

Why would the administrative sergeant at the Police Academy be affected by the Chief's growing itinerary? For some reason the Chief became enamored with the academy gym. By traditional standards, this open area with the parquet wood floor on the 6th floor of Gold Street was not a gymnasium – it was simply a large open space. It was probably the only location the Chief had visited that was large enough to hold the meetings and conferences he was planning. Since the 6th floor gym was part of the academy, my job as administrative sergeant was instantly expanded to include maître de and event planner. Whenever someone from the Chief's office would call to reserve the space, it was my responsibility to ensure that the room was set up properly and that there were the proper refreshments available. I discussed this role in greater detail in *Dark Knights*, with some of the more memorable highlights being having to supply my wife to play the piano at a promotion ceremony and supplying Russian pasties for a reception for police officials from Moscow. To this day, I am bewildered by that menu selection. If I visited Moscow, would I expect a box of Dunkin Donuts at the reception?

The receptions and conferences were coming to the 6th floor at a fast and furious pace. The one event that I could count on every week, however, was the Chief's command staff meeting where he assembled all the members of the department in the rank of captain and above.

Just inside the lobby of 300 Gold Street was, in my opinion, the world's slowest elevator. It took forever for the doors to open, and no matter how many times the "close doors" button was pressed, it seemed like an eternity before the door would actually close. Then, after an abnormally long wait the elevator would ever so slowly begin its trek up or down. The cruelest prank to play was to hit all the floor buttons from 2 to 6 while the elevator was in the lobby. With the elevator stopping at every floor it would literally take twenty minutes to make the journey to the 6th floor. Gold street regulars knew to avoid the lobby elevator like the plague. Even if using stairs was more distasteful than the slow elevator, there was still another option. At the south end of the building was another elevator. This elevator operated at a normal speed but it was very small. It could not have been much more than four feet by four feet, making two occupants the beginning of a crowding condition.

The Police Academy occupied the 4th, 5th, and 6th floors. Classrooms and offices were on the 4th and 5th floors while the aforementioned gym occupied the entire 6th floor. Whenever I was looking to move around the floors by elevator, it became an involuntary reflex to go to the small back elevator.

In one instance I was on the 4th floor, waiting for the small elevator to take me down to the lobby. When I entered the car and hit the lobby button, I was surprised to feel the elevator rising. Obviously, someone above me had called the elevator before me. As the elevator continued to the 6th floor I remembered that the Chief's command staff meeting was probably about to terminate. The door opened on the 6th floor and in marched the Chief and the two-star Assistant Chief Commanding Officer of the Inspectional Services Division. I just mentioned that two people in this tiny elevator was uncomfortable. Three people was an actual crowd.

The Chief and the Assistant Chief jammed in on either side of me. I was standing with my back pushed up against the rear elevator wall with the Chief on my left shoulder and the Assistant Chief on my right shoulder. Even though our bodies were actually touching, they never acknowledged my presence. Under the circumstances, however, this lack of recognition was understandable.

What were these circumstances? Well, obviously there would be no opportunity for the Chief to extend any social graces to a sergeant inside a cramped elevator when he was focused on assaulting the Assistant Chief. That's right – assault, and not just the verbal variety. To this day, I do not know what it was all about, but I do know what was happening mere inches away from me. The Chief was verbally blasting the Assistant Chief for something he either did or didn't do. As the verbal assault continued, the Chief began shoving the Assistant Chief on his chest with his right hand. The shoves didn't move the Assistant Chief much because there was no room for his body to move backward. This scene was surreal. What was I supposed to do if the Assistant Chief shoved back at the Chief, or if the Chief upped the ante and took a swing at the Assistant Chief? Suddenly, the door opened on the 4th floor and without a word I bladed my body, slid past the two chiefs and was gone. For the next few weeks I exclusively used the stairs.

Sgt. Bill's New Shoes

If you read *Dark Knights*, you may remember the stories about the famous Lt. Bill. Well, before there was a Lt. Bill, it was Sgt. Bill. I went through the academy with Bill, but I did not know him well. My first real association came when we were assigned as sergeants at the New York City Police Academy. I had been detailed to the academy six months before Sgt. Bill, so when Bill arrived, I assumed the role of getting him oriented. Part of that orientation was assisting him to find a locker.

At that time the NYPD Police Academy was located on East 20th Street in the Gramercy Park section of Manhattan. There were two staff locker rooms, and there was an internal subculture and pecking order regarding locker assignments. There was a staff locker room on the sixth floor, which was on the same floor as all the academic and administrative offices. This was the most desirable locker room due to its close proximately to all the staff offices. The other staff locker room was on the third floor. There was nothing wrong with this locker room except for the fact that it was directly across from the recruit cafeteria. If an instructor was using the gym or going outside to run, they would usually have to wade through a hallway filled with recruits to get into their locker room.

Since recruit classes were usually conducted in January and July, personnel changes were also usually made semi-annually. In between every class there were always instructors transferring out of and into the academy. This time period was key for locker movement. Those staff members with lockers on the third floor would pay close attention to outgoing personnel from the sixth-floor locker room. As soon as a sixth-floor locker opened up, it was a race to snap a lock onto the vacant locker before leisurely making the move from the third to the sixth floor. One such lucky staff member was Police Officer Joe, a recruit law instructor. On the same day that Sgt. Bill arrived at the academy, Joe was able to move out of the third floor and into a desirable sixth-floor locker. When it was time in the orientation to help Bill find a locker, I didn't even waste the energy of looking on the sixth floor. Instead, I took Bill directly to the third floor where I knew there would be several freshly vacated lockers. Sure enough, Bill had his choice of at least six empty lockers, and ne snapped his combination lock onto a locker in the third row.

  Before I continue, you have to understand something about the nature of Sgt. Bill. He possessed many unique attributes, but one of his more dominating features was his tendency to be – let's say – thrifty. To give you an idea of his thriftiness, Bill would always look for loose change under the cushions of the chairs in the staff lounge. Additionally, he would regularly buy his shoes by tracing his feet on a piece of paper and sending the paper off to somewhere in China where he would receive new shoes for $5.99. I think you get the picture. So, I helped Bill bring his boxes to his new locker and stayed with him while he put his uniforms and equipment inside. Suddenly, Sgt. Bill noticed something. On top of his locker were a pair of highly shined black uniform shoes. Bill's eyes lit up. "Look at this," he said as he examined his lucky find. His demeanor became even more upbeat. "They're my size too."

I didn't want to rain on his parade, but I had to point out the obvious. "They probably belong to someone who just moved up to the sixth floor and forgot the shoes were on the top of the locker."

Bill was undeterred. "You know the old saying – finders' keepers." Sgt. Bill proceeded to change into the uniform of the day, complete with his newly obtained shoes. Bill closed his locker and snapped his lock shut. We were moving down the aisle when Police Officer Joe entered the locker room and went directly to Sgt. Bill's new locker. He looked around and stroked his chin, a perplexed look on his face.

"What's wrong, Joe?" I asked.

"I just moved up to the sixth floor and I can't find my uniform shoes. I could have sworn I left them on top of my old locker."

I looked at Sgt. Bill, and to his credit, he was not going to try to hide his new acquisition. Very nonchalantly, he stated, "Oh, I found them Joe."

Now, personally, I would have been mortified to have been caught wearing another cop's uniform shoes. I never would have taken his shoes in the first place, but if I had momentarily lost my mind, I would have waited until Joe left and then put the shoes back on top of the locker. But the circumstances didn't seem to bother Sgt. Bill in the least. When he acknowledged finding he shoes, Joe said, "That's great – where are they?"

Without missing a beat, Bill smiled, pointed down and said, "I'm wearing them."

The perplexed look Joe wore moments earlier paled in comparison to his present expression, and his confusion only grew as Bill removed the shoes from his feet and handed them to him. Police Officer Joe didn't say another word as he walked out of the locker room carrying his shoes. As for Sgt. Bill, he returned to his locker sans shoes, and retrieved the pair that really belonged to him – or at least I think they belonged to him. Who knows where they may have been poached from.

I'll Get You for This

I was promoted to Lieutenant in 1993. During the two-week training school, the promotees received their new command assignments. I was on my way to District 4 in Manhattan. I wasn't overly thrilled about this assignment. I had worked in District 4 as both a cop and sergeant, and I was really looking forward to something different. Additionally, I found supervising close friends a bit uncomfortable, and most of these friends were still in the district.

Looney Larry H. was in my promotion class. I was one of the few people who would actually talk to Larry, and one day after lunch, we were sitting in the classroom waiting for afternoon training to begin. We had received our assignments during the morning, and Larry was livid about his assignment to District 12. The District 12 station house was located upstairs in the East 180th Street station in the Morris Park section of the East Bronx. Along with District 11, District 12 covered the entire subway system in the Bronx. The Bronx Borough Command was also housed inside District 12.

Larry's rant concerned the fact that he did not want to go to District 12 because he had made a complaint against a captain who worked in the borough command. Larry having a personnel problem? That was a huge surprise - not! The captain who Larry had the problem with was affectionately known as "Stinky." So, here I am, sitting at a desk in the classroom paging through a newspaper, listening to Larry ramble on about "Stinky" this and

"Stinky that, and how Stinky will get him within two weeks of his arrival. I looked up from the paper to express a bit of empathy. "That's a shame Larry. I would have loved to have been assigned to 12."

My first sentence had simply been an effort to get Larry to shut up, but my second sentence expressed my true feelings. As I previously mentioned I wasn't excited about going to District 4. Additionally, I lived in eastern Queens, and the commute to District 12 was actually much easier than traveling to Lower Manhattan. Besides, Captain Joe, the commanding officer of District 12, was a friend. There would naturally be a greater comfort level going into a new working environment under the command of someone I was familiar with.

Larry was like a snake coiled to strike. "Are you serious?" His eyes were bulging.

"Well, yeah," I responded, not knowing where he was going with this.

"When we finish today, can you walk over to Jay Street with me?"

We were taking our promotional training at a Transit Police building at 300 Gold Street in downtown Brooklyn. Transit Police headquarters was located a few blocks away at 370 Jay Street. At 4:20 PM I accompanied Larry into the NYC Transit Police Personnel Division at Jay Street. Captain Ron spoke a thousand words without opening his mouth. His face said it all. Captain Ron had established a cottage industry in adjudicating complaints made by and against

Larry, so his unannounced appearance at the Captain's door resulted in a very clear *Oh no - not him again* expression.

Larry immediately went into his non-stop, monotone diatribe regarding how it was not fair to send him into a hostile work environment in the Bronx. Captain Ron buried his head in his hands, looking very much like a man who had suddenly developed a splitting headache. He ran his hand across his forehead, took a deep breath and looked directly at me. "You want to go to District 12?"

I shrugged my shoulders, "Sure."

Captain Ron buried his head in one hand while shooing us away with the other. "Alright, I'll take care of it. Just go."

The day before the promotional school ended, my orders were changed to District 12. On that same day during lunch hour I received a disturbing phone message. Deputy Inspector M. was the commanding officer of District 4. I did not know him, but I knew he had a very good reputation as a cop and a leader. He also had a reputation for having a very dry, biting sense of humor. I was surprised and anxious when I received the message to call D.I. M. The call went something like this.

"Hello Inspector, this is Bob Bryan - one of the newly promoted lieutenants returning your call."

"Oh yeah, Bryan - I wanted to talk to you."

Deputy Inspector M. sounded upbeat. Perhaps I was anxious for nothing.

"What can I do for you, sir?"

His voice remained upbeat. "I just wanted to let you know that I am going to get you for this."

"Excuse me, sir?"

"That's right, now I have to deal with that screwball Larry as one of my lieutenant's - so I'll get you for this."

I had no idea what to say, so I said nothing.

"Have a good day, Lieutenant Bryan." Click.

What had just happened? Was he serious? Was it a dry joke? I never found out. I never had the opportunity to work for D.I. M. during the remainder of my career, and he never did get me, so I guess I'll never know the true intent of that call.

I Love a Parade

Some cities and towns in the United States have parades a few times a year to commemorate very special days and events. New York City has parades every week, with some weekends having multiple events. I know what you're thinking. I must be exaggerating, right? How can there be that many parades? Most people share this sentiment. When they start writing down each parade, their list usually doesn't get much further than the St. Patrick's Day Parade, The Thanksgiving Day Parade, The Puerto Rican Day Parade, and the Columbus Day Parade. How could we possibly get this list over fifty? Well, if you start listing events like the Hunts Point Fish Parade, the Tug Boat Races Parade, and the Topless Parade, our list quickly grows. Only in New York.

One of the more well-known parades takes place each year on Labor Day. The West Indian Day Parade has long made headlines in the city for both positive and negative reasons. On one hand, politicians and supporters of the parade will refer to the event as a beautiful, powerful expression of culture. Don't get me wrong. I'm not disputing this assessment. For many years, however, long before the parade had received so much publicity, cops always understood the violence associated with the parade. In this politically correct society, it was rather shocking a few years ago when the New York City Police Commissioner made a statement calling the West Indian Day Parade the most violent public event in the city. Sadly, it took a stray bullet to the head of an aide to the Governor of New York to prompt such a potentially "Controversial" statement from the commissioner. I'm sure I was not alone in saying that I hated working that parade on Eastern Parkway in Brooklyn.

Reflecting back, all I can think was that my financial situation must have been disastrous in 1993, because I actually volunteered to work the parade detail on overtime. Talk about blood money. I was assigned to Eastern Parkway and Utica Avenue with a sergeant and six cops. This may seem like significant numbers, but when the crowd swells to over one million, every inch of space becomes like Times Square on New Year's Eve. Cops could be packed close together yet still unable to see each other through the mass of humanity. I quickly assessed the situation and directed my squad to stay together in a very tight group. This strategy was merely a grasp at self-preservation. At the height of the afternoon, it was in the high 90s in the street and at least 110-degrees downstairs in the subway station. It didn't seem possible with the masses of people packed together that anyone would be able to do anything, no less fight. Nevertheless, fights sprung up everywhere and seemed to be non-stop. Women would suddenly begin beating each other with their shoes, while men beat each other with their fists and anything they could get their hands on. People began stripping naked for no apparent reason, other than being in the "Festive" spirit. Gangs of teenagers pushed through the throng, throwing rocks and bottles, and snatching bags and necklaces. It was absolute chaos. The situation had become an exercise in survival. There was no thought of actually making arrests – just surviving. As the sun began to go down there was a momentary lull in the action. Everyone knew this was just the calm before the storm because the violence was only going to get worse after dark. It was time to assess casualties. My uniform was completely sweat-soaked and I had lost a button on my shirt. Not bad, considering the pandemonium. Two cops in my squad had tears in the shirts, but the bottom line was that everyone was in one piece. For the moment, there were less people in the subway station, so I took my squad down to the mezzanine to take a deep breath and regroup. I gave one of the cops a few dollars and told him to go to a nearby vendor and get cold sodas for the squad. It took about ten seconds for me to drain that cold drink. Two cops apparently wanted to savor their refreshments and were still slowly sipping their sodas long after the rest of us had discarded the empty bottles in the trash.

Over the years I had several interactions with Captain A. In each case he succeeded in convincing me he was an asshole. So, when Captain A. stepped off the train at Utica Avenue I certainly wasn't going to be disappointed. He walked right up to me, but then stopped and turned from right to left, taking in the appearance of my squad. Maybe I was wrong in my prior assessment. Maybe he was going to show empathy and say that we looked like we had been through a war. Maybe he was going to suggest that we find someplace to get off our feet for a few minutes. Instead, he pointed toward the two cops still holding sodas and said, "Lieutenant, why are those officers drinking sodas?"

I believed a purely physiological answer was in order. "Because they are thirsty, sir." Captain A. obviously had no concern for proper hydration. "It is a violation of the department manual to be drinking a soda in public in uniform."

I suppose I should have been satisfied with the knowledge that I was a good judge of character.

The Soda Man

Whenever new sergeants or lieutenant's come into a command, the musical chairs begin. Personnel looking to work different hours or assignments put in requests, and new assignments are made leaving any assignments not filled for the new blood. When I arrived at District 12, I was assigned to day tours with Sundays and Mondays off. That schedule suited me fine. As a matter of fact, if I had been given a choice to pick whatever schedule I wanted, day tours would have been my choice.

My first day at District 12 I relieved Lt. Jim as the desk officer. Lt. Jim was a very affable fellow who worked steady midnights and already had over twenty years on the job. Other than a handshake, a welcome aboard, and a quick assessment that all was quiet in the command, I did not get much from Lt. Jim on that first morning. He apologized and said he couldn't hang around at all because he had to get to his second job. I jumped right into the required desk officer duties and inspections with the assistance of my assistant desk officer, Police Officer Nancy. Nancy was an extremely valuable resource. She had been on the job for eight years, all of them assigned to District 12. She knew everything about the personnel, geography, and administration of the command.

About 10am things were very quiet inside the command. I had momentarily stopped quizzing Nancy about the workings of the command because I was already risking information overload. I needed to let the information I had obtained sink in before soliciting more.

There was a CCTV camera focused on the stairs that led up to the entrance door to the command. Directly above the door a 19-inch black and white monitor was mounted, allowing the desk officer to observe visitors on the stairs before they entered the station house. My eyes were drawn to the monitor and the lone figure slowly working his way up the stairs. His slow progress was caused by his necessity to back up the stairs while he pulled a load of something on a hand jack one step at a time.

"Who's that?" I asked Nancy.

"Oh, that's just the vending machine guy. He comes a couple of times a week to fill up the soda and candy machines."

The short man in work clothes gave a quick nod toward the desk as he rolled his hand jack filled with cases of soda past the desk and into the muster room. He made several trips to replenish the machines, and each time he passed the desk I had the feeling that I knew this man. After his last trip to the machines, the man briefly stopped at the desk and gave Nancy a copy of the inventory he had stocked the machines with. He placed two cans of Coke on the desk, presumably for Nancy and me. Great, my first day in the command and I was already taking payoffs from vendors.

"Have a good day," he mumbled as he passed through the door.

As I watched the man on the monitor navigate down the stairs, it suddenly occurred to me why he may look familiar.

"Hey Nancy, that soda machine guy looks a lot like the midnight lieutenant I relieved this morning, doesn't he?"

Nancy raised her eyebrows and looked at me over her reading glasses. "Well, I would hope so, Lou. That is Lt. Jim."

"What?"

"That's his second job," Nancy continued. "He has a vending machine route."

I was totally perplexed. "How can a lieutenant in this command also own the vending machines here?"

Nancy looked down at a newspaper and shrugged. "I just work here, Lou."

I looked away from Nancy and focused on the can of coke sitting in front of me. I would have to remember to mention to Lt. Jim tomorrow morning that I drink Diet Coke.

New York Transit Police

Department Manual

Chapter 2

Section 79.0

Sub. B – No officer or employee of the department shall act as attorney, agent, broker or employee for any person, firm or corporation interested directly or indirectly, in any matter whatsoever, in business dealings with the Transit Authority.

Oh well!

Happy Cyrus Day

My birthday is September 2nd, but for a core group of colleagues, the day will forever be known as "Cyrus Day" (Remember -I can't use the real name of the person involved). District 12 was located at Morris Park Avenue and East 180th Street in the Morris Park section of the Bronx. As a lieutenant on the second platoon (day tour), it was my privilege to be directly supervising Sergeant Cyrus. Cyrus was 54-years old with more than thirty years on the job, and he lived about five minutes away from the command. Having spent most of his career in District 12, it would seem obvious that Cyrus was the wise old sage of the command, the steady old veteran hand who always would know how to keep the ship on a true course. That should have been the case, but the reality was that Cyrus was somewhat of a buffoon. A very nice man, but a buffoon nonetheless.

Cops being cops – they knew how to push Cyrus's buttons to drive him crazy, and some of the decisions he made would drive the cops and the lieutenants nuts. So, now we come to my birthday. I'm working until 4PM and I don't want to get involved with anything that is going to keep me after the tour and stop me from celebrating with my family. It is also important to note that during this period of time, the job was going through a huge "Ka-Ching" period (I believe that is how you would write the sound a cash register makes). For a variety of reasons, both internal and external, overtime had exploded. It was to a point that without any prior approval, an overtime farebeat sweep could be performed after every shift. As long as a sergeant or lieutenant had at least two cops, they could go out to a station and arrest farebeats. Every cop took two arrests, so it was very simple math. If the sweep was performed with two cops – four prisoners came back to the command; three cops – six prisoners -you get the picture. During that era, it was extremely easy to find farebeats at most of the stations in the Bronx. Once a sweep team got on the station, it would usually be a matter of minutes before they had their bodies in custody and were on their way back to the command. Everyone looked at these end of tour sweeps as easy money. The cops were allowed four hours to process their prisoners and the supervisor sat back and supervised. Most of the prisoners were issued desk appearance tickets and were released from the command to appear in court on a future date. Any prisoners found to have an active warrant were processed as keepers and were sent through the system to central booking and arraignment, with a likely overnight stay in jail. Someone in the sweep team volunteered to take any keepers and the additional overtime hours that went along with that task. The rest of the team was more than satisfied with the four hours allotted for the sweep and prisoner processing.

An unofficial tactic employed by the supervisors in the command was to get the sweep team out early whenever possible. The theory for the sergeants and lieutenants supervising the sweep was that the sooner the team returned to the district with the prisoners, the sooner the supervisor could begin watching television. I guess there were other operational reasons for this tactic. Transit Police districts had two cars assigned, so prisoner transportation could become a time-consuming issue. If a supervisor had a sweep with five cops, that meant ten prisoners had to be transported to the command. With only two cars to do the transports this task could take a very long time. And if the cars were tied up on assignments, the sweep team and their prisoners could sit on the station for hours waiting for transportation. The commanding officer of the district had made his rules crystal clear. Everyone could receive four hours overtime for a sweep, even though he was well aware that prisoners could be processed in half the time. By the same token, if the team got delayed on the station for an extended period of time waiting for transportation, and it ended up taking them a total of five hours to finish prisoner processing, he still only wanted to see four hours on the overtime slips. So, there was a lot of motivation to get out and back quickly so that a leisurely four hours of processing could ensue.

    Sometimes, you had to use ingenuity to overcome the situation. During one sweep I was supervising, my team had ten prisoners within twenty minutes of arriving on the station. Both cars were tied up on jobs, and there was no indication as to when we may be able to begin the prisoner transportation process. We were not supposed to transport prisoners on the trains, but here were my options. I could keep my ten prisoners on the station for hours waiting for the cars to become available, or I could utilize good old fashioned common sense. The station we were on was one stop from the command. I directed my team to march their prisoners to the rear of the platform. When the train arrived my cops and prisoners boarded the last car of the train. While three of the team stood guard on the prisoners, the other two members of the team ushered the riders in the car forward, out of the last car. Two minutes later, the team was walking their prisoners into the district – success.

The prisoner transportation issue was solved with the arrival of the prisoner transport vehicle. All the transit police districts received a truck with a secure rear compartment for transportation of up to ten prisoners. Prisoner transportation during sweeps became a non-issue. The sweep team simply parked the prisoner transport vehicle at the station where they were sweeping and drove the prisoners back to the command when the sweep was completed. The sweep team would usually sit in the prisoner compartment for the ride to the sweep station, while the supervisor and one cop would transport the prisoners back, with the rest of the team taking the train back to the district.

I know this was a long detour, but finally we are back to my birthday at approximately 3:15PM – 45-minutes before I can head home to celebrate. Sgt. Cyrus was going to supervise the end of tour overtime farebeat sweep, and he had assembled his three-man team, so they could get out to the selected station early. Cyrus and the three cops departed the district to get the prisoner transport vehicle and drive to their station. Specifically, Cyrus drove the vehicle while the cops were locked in the rear prisoner compartment. It was about 3:50PM when the lieutenant from the 4x12 tour came to relieve me at the desk. Before I could make my escape, the call came in. On the phone was the NYPD Bronx duty captain who calmly explained that I needed to come to the local precinct immediately to deal with a serious issue. Why did I have to ruin my birthday celebration and rush to the precinct? Well, if you guessed it had something to do with Cyrus, you'd be right. If you also guessed that it had something to do with his farebeat sweep, you'd be dead wrong. Cyrus never made it to the station. I mentioned earlier that Cyrus lived in the neighborhood of the district. I should also mention that Cyrus owned a single-family home and that he illegally rented the basement to a tenant. It seemed that Cyrus was having issues with his tenant paying the rent, so he decided to make a quick pit stop at his home to collect the rent. While he left the prisoner transport van running with the three cops locked in the back, Cyrus went into his house to confront his tenant. Apparently, the interaction didn't go well, with Mrs. Cyrus claiming that the tenant threatened her and the tenant claiming that Cyrus threatened to shoot him. The tenant called 911 and NYPD cars from the precinct began rushing up to the house. Meanwhile, the three cops are still locked inside the prisoner transport vehicle. Cell phones were around at the time, but not yet common. None of the cops had a phone, and they did not want to get on their portable radios to say that they were locked in the prisoner truck in front of the sergeant's home. The duty captain arrived and decided to bring all parties back to the precinct to sort things out. Cyrus and his wife went in one of the NYPD cars. Just as he was being driven away, Cyrus finally remembered that he had three cops locked in the prisoner vehicle.

The cops returned to the district in the prisoner transport vehicle and I received the call from the duty captain.

When I arrived at the precinct, the captain was being exceptionally gracious. He was basically making the whole scene a non-incident. The tenant realized he could face consequences, so he just wanted to forget the whole thing. One would think that Sgt. Cyrus would be chomping at the bit to put the incident behind him. After all, he went home without permission with a department vehicle, leaving three cops locked in the prisoner compartment. He confronted a tenant in his illegal rental apartment and allegedly threatened to shoot him. Who wouldn't be happy to have this go away? Well, everyone except Cyrus. Sweet old Cyrus would not stop mouthing off at the precinct desk officer and the duty captain. Finally, the gracious demeanor of the captain was gone. He said, "Lieutenant, you have exactly 30-seconds to get that lunatic out of here before I lock him up."

My driver was a big, young cop who was 6' 4" and at least 250lbs. He seemed to be stunned watching this ridiculous scene unfold in front of him. I knew I had one chance to make an exit, so I stated in my most authoritative voice, "Sgt. Cyrus, come with me, now!" Cyrus did not immediately stop ranting, so I calmly turned to my driver and said, "Ken, get the sergeant out of here, now. Carry him if you have to." The sight of the huge cop lumbering towards him finally shocked Cyrus to his senses and he stomped out of the precinct.

After an abbreviated birthday celebration, I returned for work the next morning. In the muster room, ready to turn out the day tour was smiling Sgt. Cyrus – the picture of calm tranquility. To this day, one of the sergeants from District 12 still calls me or emails me on my birthday. But he doesn't say happy birthday. The message I get is "Happy Cyrus Day."

A Little Hungry

As I mentioned in the previous story, my time as a lieutenant in District 12 was most notable for the amount of overtime available. The overtime was so plentiful, it took me until I made full pay after three years as a captain to surpass my earnings as a lieutenant in District 12. On every tour a sergeant or lieutenant could take a team out on overtime for a farebeat sweep, the only parameter being that the supervisor had to have a minimum of two cops to conduct the sweep. I was working steady day tours, and the other lieutenant and sergeants on the shift weren't that interested in the sweeps, so I was banging out these overtime sweeps several times each week. There was so much overtime for the cops, sometimes it was difficult to find two cops willing to go out on the post-tour sweep. Sometimes I would have to literally beg and or threaten cops at the morning roll call to get a team for the afternoon.

As far as I was concerned, these sweeps were easy overtime. Each cop working the sweep had to make two farebeat arrests. Even with five cops on the sweep, at most of the District 12 stations, it would take about fifteen minutes for all the cops to get their two bodies – then it was back to the district to process the arrests. Everyone, including the sweep supervisor, was good for four hours overtime for a sweep, and one cop was designated for "keepers," and made additional overtime processing any of the arrestees who could not be issued desk appearance tickets because they had a warrant. Once we were back in the command, my job was to supervise my sweep team, which meant I usually watched TV while my cops processed their arrests. When the arrest paperwork was completed, I reviewed and signed the forms, and the prisoner was released with an appearance ticket to appear in court on a future date. When all the prisoners were processed and released, we all filled out the forms for our four hours of overtime and went home – this is a great country.

One of the main reasons the supervisor was allowed to make overtime was to take some of the load off the district desk officer. In every command, a sergeant or lieutenant is assigned as the desk officer and is responsible for all operations in the command during the tour. There was usually enough for the desk officer to keep track of during a shift without thrusting ten prisoners from a farebeat sweep on him or her. Everybody was usually happy. The desk officer did not have to be concerned with the farebeat sweep prisoners and I could make my overtime.

There was one particular sweep where I had to beg during the morning roll call, and I was ultimately able to come up with two cops to sweep with me at the end of the tour. We went out at the end of the tour and were back with four bodies within a half hour. Lieutenant Joe was the desk officer on the 4 x 12 tour. Joe had been in my recruit company during academy training, and during this tour he had his hands full with a very busy district and several prisoners, besides my sweep farebeats, in the cells. One of the prisoners already in the cells when I returned with my sweep was a real transit felon. This guy looked like Lon Chaney in the old Wolfman movies when he was about half way through his transformation from man to wolf. This man-beast had the audacity to be urinating on the platform at the Bronx Park East station, and since the young cop attempting to issue the summons had no silver bullets handy, he had to engage in hand to hand combat with this moron when it became clear that he was not enthusiastic about receiving the summons. Ultimately, good triumphed over evil, and now, this lunatic was literally growling and howling inside the cell. When I arrived at the command with my sweep prisoners, Lt. Joe told me to house my prisoners in the other cell. He had the howling man-wolf alone in the second cell, handcuffed to the bars so he couldn't move to hurt himself – or so he thought.

One thing about being a cop is that you quickly learn to become numb to the lunacy taking place around you. It mattered not that the wolfman was growling and drooling in his private cell. My cops were busy walking back and forth getting information to process their prisoners from the farebeat sweep. About a half hour after my prisoners were lodged, I was sitting in the administrative office watching TV – I mean reviewing arrest paperwork, when one of my sweep team approached me. Police Officer Francis was a classic dark knight – a cop who could find something hysterical under the most morbid circumstances.

"Hey Lou," Francis had a huge grin on his face. "You better come see this."

I followed Francis back to the cell area where three other cops with equally huge grins were studying some activity inside one of the cells. The cops cleared out of the way, so I could get a view of the cell. There was only one thing I could say. "Holy Shit!"

The wolfman was like a man who hadn't eaten for days, enjoying a Thanksgiving feast, only it wasn't a turkey leg he was gnawing on – it was his own arm. Blood was squirting everywhere as this guy attempted to free himself from the handcuff by chewing off his own arm. He was actually doing a pretty good job. I never saw anything like it. My next reaction was to be thankful that the beast wasn't one of my sweep prisoners. I told one of my cops to go to the desk and get Lt. Joe to come back here forthwith.

"What's up?" Joe stated as he approached. All I did was smile and point, prompting Joe to respond exactly as I did. "Holy Shit!"

Joe looked at me. "What are we gonna do?"

I was very tempted to say, "What do you mean WE, paleface." but that wouldn't have been right.

I was blunt and to the point. "I'm not sending any of my cops in there to get chewed on by that lunatic, so I guess we better call EMRU."

The Transit Police had their own version of the NYPD Emergency Services Unit called the Emergency Medical Rescue Unit. EMRU was as skilled as ESU, but there was routinely only one truck operating citywide, so there could be an extended waiting time for EMRU. With no ETA for EMRU, Joe called for ESU. When the ESU truck arrived, the cops took one look at the wolfman and went back to their truck and broke out the EDP blanket. EDP stands for emotionally disturbed person, and this device was like a very heavy blanket that fully enveloped the EDP, with only his head sticking out from the top. When the wolfman was carried out of the command, howling into the night, PO Francis rubbed his hands together and queried everyone gathered around the district desk. "OK, who wants to order dinner?" Like I said, you quickly become numb to what goes on around you.

Pasty Boy

When I was first assigned to the NYPD Police Academy as an instructor, I had to complete a two-week methods of instructions course. As I previously mentioned, the main instructor for the MOI likened police training to a rubber band. He said that once a police officer was involved in police training, the rubber band became firmly attached, and throughout a career the rubber band would keep pulling you back to the police academy. As a lieutenant, the rubber band had the elasticity remaining for one last pull, this time not to the NYPD Police Academy, but to the Transit Police Academy located in Brooklyn at 300 Gold Street. By the time I landed at Gold Street, the Transit Police was in a state of denial. As it became clearer that the merger with the NYPD would be inevitable, the Transit Police Department continued to take steps to distance themselves from the NYPD. One such step was to pull out of the NYPD Police Academy and establish a police academy with recruit training at Gold Street. The Transit Police Department even convinced the Long Island Railroad and Metro North Police Departments (subsequently to become the MTA Police Department) to also pull away from the NYPD and train at Gold Street.

When the rubber band pulled me from the Bronx to Gold Street, I did not land in the recruit training school. The Transit Police had other specialized training operations, and I became the commanding officer of the Educational Development Unit, or EDU. EDU was responsible for all the in-service, promotional, and specialized training in the Transit Police Department.

Throughout my increasingly long life, there are very few people that I truly dislike. In fact, there is only one person who I can say that I dislike to the point that I wish him bad fortune. That person was Sgt. D., and he was a member of EDU. I had a long negative history with Sgt. D. for which I would likely need Dark Knights 4 to really get into. Suffice to say that there was no love lost between us, but the tactical advantage had changed. When the exchange of battle first occurred, he was more heavily armed as a sergeant, while I was a police officer. Now, however, the balance of power had shifted. I was coming to the unit as its lieutenant commanding officer while Sgt. D. was still a sergeant. I was honestly going to let bygones be bygones, but Sgt. D. must have been in a panic, because the day before my arrival he was transferred out of EDU to the special projects section of the academy. More on Sgt. D. in a bit.

My crew at EDU consisted of four police officers and three sergeants, all very competent trainers. There were, however, some extremely quirky personalities within the staff. Take Police Officer Pete, for example. Pete was the model for a police trainer. A Marine Captain with exceptional writing and public speaking skills. Too good to be true, right? The big emergency door investigation took over two months to solve. Several times a week in the late afternoon the audible alarm on the emergency exit door at the rear of the building on Flatbush Avenue would activate. There was a police officer assigned to building security at a lobby reception desk, but whenever the officer would respond to the alarm there was no sign of how the alarm activated. There were no CCTV cameras by the door at the time, so the question remained - why was the alarm sounding? Was it some mechanical defect or was there someone actually opening the door?

Parking for staff at Gold Street was always an issue. One of the benefits of being the commanding officer of a unit was that I received a parking space inside the very small parking lot in the front of the building. There was very little parking on Gold Street, and most staff members had to park on the street several blocks away. As previously mentioned, the rear of the building bordered Flatbush Avenue, and there was metered parking along the stretch next to the building. With Flatbush Avenue being a major road for access to both the Manhattan and Brooklyn Bridges, the parking meters only became legal after 10am. With my training operations, most of my staff worked early day tours, either 7am x 3pm or 8am to 4pm, but I had to have coverage in the office until 6pm. PO Pete would usually be my 10am x 6pm staff member. It was tough enough getting parking in the early morning. A 10am start would require parking even further from the building. There was a silver lining for PO Pete in the 10am start. Parking in the meters on Flatbush Avenue became legal. He could easily find a meter, and his PBA card in the windshield would virtually guarantee that he would not receive a summons for an expired meter. Who had it better than officer Pete? Well, evidently, officer Pete figured out a way that he could have it even better. One day, in the midst of the unsolved emergency door alarm mystery, Captain K, the commanding officer of the recruit school was working a later tour, and at 6PM he had decided to take a walk to get something to eat. The path of his walk took him to Flatbush Avenue, adjacent to the rear of the building. What a surprise it must have been to the good captain when his casual stroll was interrupted by the sound of a loud alarm buzzer followed by a figure barreling through the emergency door and continuing in a sprint along the sidewalk. The captain took note that the sprinter entered a parked vehicle and sped away into the Flatbush Avenue traffic. I guess you have solved the mystery by now. It was PO Pete. Even though Pete had easy parking on Flatbush Avenue at 10AM, I guess it was just too much trouble at 6PM to exit through the front of the building and walk around the block to his car on Flatbush Avenue. Why should he go through all that trouble when he could just blast through the emergency door every afternoon and sprint to his parked car. PO Pete received a written complaint that one would think would have cured his "it's too much trouble" syndrome, but it didn't.

Log books have always been a staple of police documentation, and were used in departments all over the country because pages were sequentially numbered, making entries a permanent record. A page could not simply be torn out. Along with the type of log book, there were specific department guidelines for making entries in log books. In the Transit Police Department, all entries had to be in blue or black ink. There was also a specific format for correction. Erasing or using white out was not permitted.

Corrections were made by drawing a single line through the error, with the initials of the person making the correction written adjacent to the correction. These weren't obsolete rules. Everyone knew how to make proper log entries. Well, maybe not everyone.

The EDU command log book provided the daily staff schedule with a place for members to sign in and out. The first entries were a run-down of the daily roll call. All the names were listed with the scheduled hours they were working. At the right margin of the page were locations for the members to sign in and out. As the staff member working late, one of PO Pete's duties was to set up the log for the following day. This task involved writing the names of the members of EDU with their scheduled tours of duty. This may sound like a laborious undertaking, but remember, there were only eight members of EDU. Writing eight names with their scheduled shifts wasn't too much trouble, was it? Well, I guess when you suffered from "too much trouble syndrome," it was. PO Pete's new log book innovation happened during a week I was on vacation, and I was actually more upset with my sergeants for allowing this than I was at Pete. After all, Pete was sick with the syndrome. He must have been sick. What else would prompt a police officer to forego the procedure of writing the names in the log and instead take the book to a copy machine and copy the roll call page. Only some condition of delirium would then allow the police officer to cut out the copy of the roll call and paste it into the log book - and to paste it again the following day, and the next day. When I returned from vacation and was about to sign into the log, and saw the pasted roll call, I almost fell over. From that moment forward, PO Pete had a new nickname - Pasty Boy!

The Captain is Crazy

In-service training was always a challenge for instructors. For the most part, cops looked at the annual day of training as nothing more than a day off patrol. They certainly were not going to enthusiastically embrace most of the annual training topics that usually revolved around being courteous to the public. With the topics being so challenging, I was always open to suggestions on how to create more interest and buy-in from the trainees. During one particular training cycle, one of the topics was suicide awareness. This was a very serious topic, especially in lieu of the fact that the suicide rate among police officers was much higher than the general population. Despite the seriousness of the topic, the police officer audience was still not going to be receptive to a barrage of statistical information.

Police Officer Andy was one of the more insightful member of my staff. Andy would routinely think out of the box to come up with ideas to make the training more worthwhile. In this case, Andy had an idea on how to put a real face to the suicide statistics. Several years earlier, there had been a politician in Pennsylvania who had been caught with his hand in the cookie jar. This politician was facing jail time and had called a news conference, presumably to resign. After some opening remarks behind the podium, the man produced a large envelope and very calmly pulled a revolver out of the envelope. After a brief warning for people to stay away from him, he put the barrel in his mouth and squeezed the trigger. It was a very graphic scene and Andy had a videotape of the incident. I agreed that by beginning the suicide awareness section with this short video, there would be a captive audience for the remainder of the lecture.

Enter into the scene Captain J. Captain J. was a female out of my academy class who had been transferred into the Transit Police Academy with no other duties than to oversee EDU. The assignment made no sense. I was the commanding officer of EDU and I was still the C.O. of the unit. I now answered to Capt. J., but she had no other responsibilities besides EDU. Why would they dump a captain into that unnecessary position? Were they trying to hide her? Over the next several months the answer to that question became crystal clear. The first clue was supplied via the suicide video.

The in-service cycle began and every day from Monday through Friday we would get approximately twenty cops in an in-service class. There were about three thousand police officers in the Transit Police at the time, so it would take the better part of a year to complete an in-service training cycle. We had put about a thousand cops through the cycle and the critiques prepared by the cops after each class were exceptional as it related to the section on suicide awareness. Then one fine day I received a frantic sounding call from Captain J. to report to her office. I would come to learn that just about every call from Captain J. was frantic sounding. The captain said that she had decided to observe the in-service class, and that she was stunned to see the suicide video being shown. I explained that I failed to see the stunning nature. The video accomplished putting a real face on the tragedy of suicide. I then had one of the more classic dialogues of my twenty-year career:

Captain J: "What are we going to do if viewing that tape causes cops to commit suicide?"

Me: "What?"

Captain J: "You heard me. What if cops kill themselves because they saw the video?"

Me: "Excuse me Captain, but the best evaluations we are getting from the cops is for the suicide awareness section. And besides, we've already presented it to over a thousand cops."

Captain J.: "A thousand cops – Oh my God! What are we going to do?"

Me: "Do? Why do we need to do anything?"

Captain J.: "We need to offer counselling to every cop who saw that video before it's too late."

Me: "Are you serious?"

Captain J.: "I am completely serious, Lieutenant. I want a complete list of all the police officers who viewed that video by tomorrow."

Me: "Yes ma'am."

That bizarre conversation resulted in an immediate meeting with Sgt. Tony, who was the administrator for the current in-service training cycle. I told him to stop showing the suicide video immediately and to compile a list of those who had already completed the cycle and seen the video. Tony responded the same way I had, but I explained that common sense and reason was not winning the day, and to just begin compiling the list. At that time, compiling a list was not as simple as hitting a few keys and populating an Excel spreadsheet. The names of attendees were listed in the EDU log. Compiling a list would mean going page by page in the log for five months. The next morning when I arrived at Gold Street Sgt. Tony was ready with the list. I was impressed. There was at least thirty pages of typed names. I did not hesitate. I grabbed the list and proceeded to the Captain's office. Captain J. took the list and began to review the names. After flipping through several pages, she looked up at me,

"Who's B. Booey?"

"What?"

Captain J. pointed to the name. I grabbed the list and stared at the name. To my horror, I immediately knew what happened. Sgt. Tony had been so timely in the completion of the list because he simply made most of the names up. I don't know exactly how many names were bogus, but I recognized several fakes. Sgt. Tony and I were both big fans of the Howard Stern radio show, and he had used names from the Stern Show on his list. B. Booey was short for Baba Booey, the nickname of the show's producer.

I maintained my composure and handed the list back to Captain J. In a very nonchalant tone of voice I stated, "Booey is a cop in District 33."

I held my breath until Captain J. responded, "Oh, yes. I think I know him."

It's a Piece of Cake

As it became more apparent that the merger with the NYPD would become a reality, the Transit Police Department remained in a state of denial. This unrealistic state was no more apparent than during the final Transit Police promotion ceremony. The sixth floor at 300 Gold Street was a large open space that was used for several purposes. It was used as a gymnasium for recruit physical training, and it also served as the venue for larger meetings and events. One of my responsibilities at EDU was to run the promotional training classes for sergeants and lieutenants. EDU was not responsible for the actual promotion ceremony, but obviously, the promotions had to be closely coordinated with the training courses. This coordination was especially important because the Transit Police had no set standard for handling the promotional schools and promotion ceremony. Sometimes, promotees would be detailed to the training school first, with the actual promotion ceremony taking place at the end of the school. At other times, however, the personnel would be immediately promoted to sergeants and lieutenants respectively and then detailed to the promotional schools. This lack of standardization could result in some pretty absurd circumstances. For instance, when I was promoted to sergeant in 1988, we were detailed to the three-week promotional school first, with the promotions scheduled to take place at the end of the class. When we arrived for the sergeant's school the instructors informed us of the uniform we would need for the promotion ceremony and directed us to have sergeant stripes sewn onto all our uniform shirts. About a week before the promotion ceremony the demonstration billed as a "Day of Outrage and Mourning," had been called to protest the killing of a black youth, 16-year-old Yusuf K. Hawkins, by a gang of white youths in Bensonhurst. In the first of those protests, about 500 people halted subway and bridge traffic between Brooklyn and Manhattan and disrupted more than 700,000 commuters. Later protests were met by well-organized police tactics and caused less disruption.

Since the department felt they were caught with their pants down during the first Day of Outrage, it was primed for a complete overreaction for the next Day of Outrage that was announced for a day during the last week of our sergeant's school. Virtually every cop in the department was being sent out on patrol for this protest. But this couldn't include the cops who were currently in the middle of their promotional training course, could it? Of course not. After all, as directed, we all had sergeant's stripes on our uniform shirts, but we weren't sergeants yet. The department would never send cops wearing police officer shields out on patrol with sergeant's stripes, would they? Short answer – they would and they did.

Back to the original story. There were approximately forty promotees to the ranks of sergeant and lieutenant. Including guests and VIPs we would have around 120-150 people on the 6th floor for the ceremony. This amount of people was well within the floor's capacity, and considering the fact that promotions were always a festive event, no problems were anticipated. I did, however, fail to anticipate that Captain J. failed to take her medication on that day.

Everything went according to plan. The promotees received their new sergeant's and lieutenant's shields, speeches were made, including a particularly ludicrous speech by the man who would turn out to be the final Chief of the Transit Police Department. In his remarks, the Chief assured the audience that there would be no police merger and that the Transit Police was about to move ahead with its own crime scene unit. When the sixth-floor agenda was over, there was one final piece of business that needed to be addressed.

Sgt. F. was the administrative sergeant for the Transit Police Academy, and among his duties was the administration of police identification cards for all members of the department. Accordingly, the promotees had to receive their new sergeant's and lieutenant's ID cards before they departed the building. In retrospect, I suppose Sgt. F. could have brought his ID equipment upstairs and processed the ID cards on the 6th floor, but the process should not have been a big deal. On the 5th floor were all the academy classrooms and administrative offices. As the promotion ceremony ended, the promotees were directed to stop on the 5th floor and pick up their new ID cards. The photos had already been taken, so all that was required was for a promotee to sign the ID card log, turn in their old card and accept their new ID card. It was a very quick process, and I was actually enjoying the line of promotees and their families on the

5th floor. I knew many of these new sergeants and lieutenants and it was nice to wish them well and meet their families.

There were a lot of people on the 5th floor, but again, everyone was in great spirits and there were no problems. Suddenly, there was someone pushing through the hallway who was not in a very festive mood. I became aware of Captain J's presence when I heard her screaming my name from down the hall. When she approached me, I was very concerned. The wild look in her eyes led me to believe that some major incident had just occurred that I was unaware of. Maybe one of the family members was injured or seriously ill. All I knew was that the look in her eyes told me that something was seriously wrong. She then proceeded to scream the problem.

"Lt. Bryan, there is a serious crowd condition here."

Crowd condition? What was she talking about. There were a bunch of newly promoted sergeants and lieutenants accompanied by family members, quickly picking up their new ID cards. I tried to reassure the good captain. "No worries Captain. they are just picking up ID cards. The floor will be cleared out in a few minutes."

Her waving arms and shrill voice was clear indication of her dissatisfaction with my response. "This is a dangerous crowd. You clear this floor - NOW!"

Around the time I had received these orders, a smiling Lt. C. approached and gave me a hug. Lt. C previously worked at the academy and he was present to see his wife get promoted to sergeant. Lt. C. barely had time for the hug when Captain J. broke in. "Lt. C - leave Lt. Bryan alone. He is dealing with a dangerous crowd condition."

Lt. C. was sincerely confused. "What crowd?"

Captain J. apparently had no time to waste with explanations. She grabbed Lt. C by the right arm and began guiding him towards the stairs. "Come with me Lieutenant, I am ejecting you from the building."

The last vision I have was Lt. C's confused, laughing face as he disappeared into the stairwell.

I knew it would take several minutes for Captain J to actually throw Lt. C out the front door, so I had to use this time wisely. I called over Sgt. F. and told him that we had to get everyone back to the 6th floor immediately. Sgt. Tony asked how we were going to be able to quickly accomplish this and I told him to use his imagination. To the best of my recollection it was an academy staff member's birthday, and there was a cake on the 5th floor to celebrate the birthday. Tony never missed a beat. He picked up the large cake and yelled for everyone to follow him back up to the 6th floor because we had forgotten to have the cake to celebrate the promotions. I don't know if we ever got another cake for the birthday boy or girl.

Put in my Place

The end of what little relationship I had with Captain J. came about rather unceremoniously under the worst possible circumstances for me – with Sgt. D. looking at me with a smug, self-satisfied grin.

Chief C. was in command of all Transit Police Academy operations. Every week, the Chief would hold a staff meeting including all the components of the academy. Present at these meetings were representatives from the recruit training school, the recruitment unit, special projects, administration, as well as Captain J. and myself representing EDU. The meetings were held in a conference room where the attendees sat around a circular conference table. During this meeting, the subject of an upcoming method of instruction course had come up. Sgt. D. was responsible to administer the MOI course, and he would have to detail three instructors to special projects for the two-week course. At one point during the meeting Sgt. D. said he was going to use one of my staff members, PO Pete, for the MOI course. He didn't request or ask for my personnel, he just said he was taking him. Obviously, that didn't sit well with me, especially since it was coming from Sgt. D. I said something about checking to see if I could spare him, and Sgt. D. very arrogantly said he was taking him anyway.

At this point it is important to understand the seating arrangements. Captain J. was on my right and Sgt. D. was two seats further right. So, when I pointed my right index finger in the direction of Sgt. D. and stated emphatically that I would decide who gets detailed from my unit, my right arm was directly in front of Captain J. – in perfect position for her to slap my hand down and say, "That will be enough out of you!"

One would think that the public emasculation was the worst level of embarrassment, but having to look at the smug, wry grin on Sgt. D. was more than I could take. When the meeting ended I went directly to Dr. O's office. Dr. O was the civilian director of training at the academy, and was second in command under Chief C. Dr. O was a regular guy and I felt comfortable talking to him, so I had no problem bursting into his office and declaring that I was not going to work another day with that psychotic captain. I implored him to send me to any patrol command on any shift, but to please get me away from her. To his credit, Dr. O allowed me to vent before telling me to calm down and think about my request, and to come back to him the next day if I still felt the same way.

The next day, I was still fired up from the previous day's humiliation. I went to Dr. O's office to repeat my request for a transfer. He knew why I was there, and before I could say a word he held up his hand and smiled. "Read this," he said.

Dr. O. handed me a personnel order. I thought I was looking at my transfer, but upon examining the document I was shocked to see that it was Captain J's transfer. Let me be perfectly clear about something. The Captain's transfer had nothing to do with my ultimatum. Her transfer was coming with or without my rant to Dr. O., but as far as I was concerned, it was perfect timing.

Hee Haw

Finding a good police trainer was no easy task. It was like a food recipe. You knew what you needed, but a little too much or too little of an ingredient spoiled the entire finished product. The same principle held true for a police instructor. In a perfect world, the instructor would have years of patrol experience before venturing into the world of training. The patrol experience lent itself to credibility, and was particularly relevant to an in-service training instructor. Patrol experience was helpful in any training environment, but for recruit training, even if the instructor had only ten minutes of patrol experience, it was still ten minutes more than the recruits he/she was training. The in-service training instructor, however, was faced with a far more difficult challenge. Every day, the police officer instructor would get up in front of other police officers, most of whom were unreceptive or apathetic to the training topic. Most of the time the instructors welcomed apathy, as the alternative always seemed to be combativeness from salty veterans, who may have had all of one year on the job, who always seemed to know more than the instructor. It took a rare personality to get in front of that classroom each day and sell a product that most of the audience did not believe in, and that the instructor him or herself wasn't all that enthusiastic about.

Food recipes have more than one ingredient, and it was not enough for an instructor to be good on the platform in front of a class. Just as important as the platform skills were the writing skills. All training programs involved curriculum development. Even if some subject that no one believed in was being jammed down our throats, it wasn't jammed down there with a curriculum attached. A curriculum with lesson plans had to be developed, and that was the job of the instructors. The ability to write is not a skill inherent in being a police officer. I knew many fantastic patrol cops who could not write a coherent sentence. Additionally, writing ability does not affect the ability of an instructor to perform effectively in front of a class. As a matter of fact, I have seen many instances where an impeccable writer and researcher completely froze in front of a class. That's why if you have an in-service instructor who is effective and comfortable standing up there in front of his peers each day, handling the abuse and mixing it up in a professional and positive manner, you make allowances if he is lacking somewhat in the writing department.

  When I was transferred to EDU Police Officer Louie was already assigned to the unit. Louie had been on the job for a little over ten years, with nine of those being on patrol in Brooklyn. He had obtained a bachelor's degree by attending college part time over the past several years, and once he received his B.S. he applied for assignment to the academy. On face value, Louie seemed like a home run for the unit. A respected patrol cop is the desired recipe to get up in front of the sometimes-hostile audience in an in-service training class. And Louie did extremely well in the classroom environment. Day after day he handled the know-it-alls and naysayers. Yes, Louie was a home run – in the classroom, that is. His writing skills were another story. As the commanding officer of a unit, I always had to strive to put square pegs in square holes, so I would always have Louie in the classroom, while leaving curriculum development to others with better writing skills. In retrospect, this philosophy was a failure on my part because how would Louie ever develop writing skills If I never provided any training that would enhance his skills. My neglect of Louie's writing skills became painfully obvious during a visit to New Jersey.

The Port Authority of New York and New Jersey Police Department, or Port Authority Police Department (PAPD), is a law enforcement agency in New York and New Jersey, the duties of which are to protect and to enforce state and city laws at all the facilities, owned or operated by the Port Authority of New York and New Jersey, the bi-state agency running airports, seaports, and many bridges and tunnels within the Port of New York and New Jersey. The PAPD is the largest transit-related police force in the United States.

Approximately two years after the 1993 World Trade Center bombing I was invited to the Port Authority Police Academy to attend a week-long training course on Critical Incident Management. The course was not operational, but involved the best practices for presenting training on the topic. The Transit Police Academy was offered three seats in the class, so besides myself, I brought Sgt. Tony and Police Officer Louie. There were six other police departments at this excellent training course that was facilitated by a Port Authority Police Inspector who tragically lost his life on 9/11.

The course culminated in the presentation of a critical incident related training topic by each department. I don't recall exactly what our topic was, but I do remember that there were individual presentations. I gave a presentation on a topic, followed by Sgt. Tony on another topic, and finishing up with Police Officer Louie on yet another area. Training aids are always important to the presentation of a training course, and in that era, the visual training aids did not get much more elaborate than use of a blackboard or a flip chart. Tony, Louie and I worked together in arranging the flow of our presentations, but when it came to preparing our flip charts, we worked independently. That turned out to be a huge mistake.

Tony and I completed our presentations, and I was extremely happy with how our topic was progressing. Now it was up to Louie to tie things together and bring it home. I don't remember exactly what the scope of Louie's topic involved, but I certainly recall two areas he covered. Louie made mention of borough-based training. The NYPD and Transit Police were broken down into patrol boroughs, with some training being conducted at the borough level – in other words, borough-based. At another point in his presentation, Louie referenced Special Weapons and Tactics, usually referred to as SWAT teams. I think Louie was making the point that NYPD and Transit Police did not have SWAT units, with the NYPD equivalent being the Emergency Services Unit (ESU) and the Transit Police having the Emergency Medical Rescue Unit (EMRU).

I could not have been happier. As Louie's speech wound down I was more than satisfied with the fine account the Transit

Police Academy had given for itself in front of all these other departments. Then, it happened. Louie turned the page on his flip chart. He had reached the topic of borough based training, but staring boldly at me from the chart was BURRO based training. The representatives from the other departments were trying to be polite and hold in their laughter. They did a better job than I would have done. I wanted so badly for Louie to finish that page and flip the chart. I should have been more careful with that desire. Sometimes you get what you wish for. I breathed a sigh of relief when Louie flipped to a new page. My relief, however, was short-lived. Louie was now on his material regarding ESU, EMRU and SWAT units, but now on the fresh page, facing me in all its glory, was *THE IMPORTANCE OF SWAP TRAINING*. To make matters worse, Louie had not just made a mistake in writing SWAT. He actually thought SWAP was the correct term, and he kept repeating it over and over again. Each time he said SWAP I sunk lower and lower in my chair.

    In typical police humor fashion, Sgt. Tony took care of the inevitable follow-up. Within a day of our return to Gold Street, a new sign appeared on the wall next to Louie's desk. The sign was a 2-foot x 3-foot cut out of a donkey. On the body of the donkey was printed very neatly – PO Louie, COORDINATOR, BURRO BASED TRAINING. To his credit, Louie left the sign on the wall.

The Duty Captain

When the merger of the NYPD and Transit Police occurred on April 2, 1995, I was merged out of my position as commanding officer of the Educational Development Unit at the Transit Police Academy. All my staff was moved to the NYPD police academy, but I was transferred to patrol. I was transferred to District 20, the command that covered the subway system throughout most of Queens. Even though I was now part of the NYPD, other than the patch on my shirt, nothing had really changed. Transit police districts functioned exactly as they had before the merger, except that they were now part of the NYPD Transit Bureau.

The change of command also provided an opportunity for a reunion with "Screwy Louie." Lt. B. was now Captain B. and I would see him occasionally when he visited the command as the duty captain. Believe me, occasionally, was much more interaction than I desired to have with Captain B. Besides being a world class asshole, he was also a world class germaphobe. It was a combination of these two characteristics that provides the essence of this story.

Joe was the cleaner assigned to District 20. You could not find a more affable fellow. Joe had been a cleaner for the Transit Authority for over thirty years, and he had now been merged into the NYPD as a civilian cleaner. Joe was the type of guy who always had a smile on his face and a warm greeting. I never saw him in a bad mood. Wait a minute – make that I "almost" never saw him in a bad mood. Joe's grin quickly turned into a scowl whenever Captain B. visited the command.

Whenever I was the desk officer and Captain B. would visit, the routine was always the same. He would enter the command without saying hello, walk behind the desk to sign the blotter, then disappear into the back of the district to use the bathroom. Ten minutes later he would leave without saying goodbye. Captain B's departure was always quickly flowed by Joe walking past the desk sneering and muttering curses under his breath.

Finally, after the honor of another Captain B. visit, I had to solve the mystery of Joe's bad mood. This time, when he walked by the desk, cursing under his breath, I stopped him.

"Joe, what's wrong?"

Joe placed his hands on his hips and took a deep breath. He waved his hand toward the door Captain B. had recently passed through. "That asshole! That's what's wrong."

I chuckled, but the fact that Captain B. was an asshole was not a revelation. There had to be more.

Joe leaned on the desk, and in his thick Jamaican accent he said, "OK mon, I tell you the story. I talk to this guy every time he comes in, but he still keeps doin it."

"Doing what?"

"Every time he comes here he goes to the bathroom, and every time he leaves there's shit on the floor."

"What?"

"Dat's right, mon. The captain shits on the floor."

"Wait a minute, Joe." I held up my hand. "I think I'm missing something. Why don't you back up and start at the beginning?"

Joe took another deep breath. "When dis guy starts visiting the district – three times I find shit on the floor right after he leaves. The next time I see him come into the bathroom, I waited outside and when I see him leave I run into the stall and find shit again. I run up to the desk before he leaves and say 'why do you shit on the floor, Captain?'"

I was hysterical. "What did he say, Joe?"

"He points his finger and sneers at me and says 'I don't put my ass on those filthy, germ infested toilet seats. I stand over the bowl.' So, as he is walking out the door I yell out – at least can you aim better."

Unbelievable! Captain B. truly was the duty captain!

First Impression

The first time I really began assimilation into the NYPD was when I applied for an investigative assignment. The NYPD had a policy requiring all sergeants and lieutenants seeking assignment to an investigative bureau to submit a generic application for an investigative assignment. The catch with this system was that those supervisors accepted were automatically drafted into the Internal Affairs Bureau for two years. I was accepted and transferred into Internal Affairs Bureau Group 27, where I remained for the next two years. I did not realize it at the time, but this transfer constituted my final departure from the world of transit policing. I had worked with the NYPD before when I was detailed to the NYPD Police Academy as an instructor. During those years, however, I was a transit cop detailed to the NYPD. Now, I was just another lieutenant on the job.

Despite being part of an NYPD investigative unit, it was impossible to shake my transit roots, nor did I want to shake my roots. I was the only pre-merge member of the Transit Police assigned to Group 27, and it seemed that there was a perception among the other members of the group that I must know every person who ever worked for the transit police. It was amusing when one of the group members would ask me, "You must know my brother-in-law. He was in transit in the 70s." There was always a puzzled look when I would try to explain that I wasn't even on the job in the 1970s, and that there were over 3000 members of the transit police. Please forgive me for not being familiar with your brother-in-law.

There was, however, one very funny "You must know so and so" moment. Captain G. was the commanding officer of group 27 when I arrived in the unit. During one of our initial interactions, the conversation inevitably moved to the fact that I was formerly transit, and did I know someone. In this case, however, I did know the person the Captain was inquiring about. Captain G. Had been assigned to the 60th Precinct in Patrol Borough Brooklyn South at the time of the merger. When the merger occurred, NYPD units were directed to establish liaison with the transit commands within their geographical areas. Transit Police District 34 was located within the confines of the 60th Precinct. Specifically, the district was located in a street level building under the elevated Stillwell Avenue subway structure. Besides District 34, the Transit Brooklyn Borough Command was also located in the same building. Inspector A. was the commanding officer of Transit Borough Brooklyn. I never worked for Inspector A, but I knew of him. Specifically, I knew of the stories circulating about his bathroom habits, which I just assumed were nothing more than urban legends. The stories centered around the Inspector having a urination frequency problem. I heard stories about him urinating in stairways, out windows, and even a story about him having some device with a tube that he could quickly place over his manhood while driving. Again, I called B.S. on all these tales. A police inspector couldn't be pissing all over the place like that, could he? And then, I had the conversation with Captain G.

As the executive officer of the 60th Precinct, Captain G and several other precinct executive officers and commanding officers met in Inspector A's Stillwell Avenue office for a post-merger get acquainted meeting. Captain G said that about ten minutes into the meeting Inspector A removed an empty glass jar from his bottom desk drawer. He continued that the Inspector never broke the conversation as he proceeded to get up and walk to the corner of his office. Captain G. said that the Inspector continued his normal conversation as he unzipped his fly and urinated into the jar. As the shocked attendees watched with wide eyes and open mouths, Capt. G said that Inspector A then nonchalantly walked to the window behind his desk and poured the urine out the window. He then returned to his chair and continued with the meeting. If I try to put a positive spin on this incident, it is good to leave an impression on people during a first meeting, isn't it?

The Afterlife

"Nothing is certain except death and taxes." We've all heard the quote. It's cemented a place in our history and popular culture. Who came up with this commentary on life? Was it Benjamin Franklin or Mark Twain? There has been much debate over who actually coined the phrase first. What is without controversy, however, is the veracity of the words. It is safe to assume that we live in a world where taxation in some form will always exist, and we need make no assumptions about our mortality. One day we will all lift the veil of our mortal existence and move on. Move on to what? That answer depends on your belief system. Is it paradise or damnation? Is it recycling to a different life or is it simply non-existence? Whatever it is, one thing is certain. When we die, our physical lives here are over, so something happens to us after this life. Whether it is paradise or non-existence, there is something that follows – an afterlife.

Stop looking at the cover of the book. The previous chapters of this book were not a ploy to deliver a religious or philosophical message. This is a police book, and in this final section I take the last logical step in a police career – the afterlife. Let me be clear, this chapter has nothing to do with police officers killed in the line of duty. There is absolutely nothing humorous about the ultimate sacrifice made by these heroes. The afterlife I am referring to is life after the job.

Law enforcement is a unique profession in many ways. The afterlife becomes a more meaningful issue for cops because there is usually the potential to retire at a very young age. A typical retired police officer may be in his or her early forties, with virtually a whole lifetime still ahead. For a vast majority of officers, particularly in the NYPD, the 20-year retirement date is a milestone they yearn for. They can receive their pensions while starting second careers in the private industry, or working for police agencies in states that hire older officers.

Many have it down to the exact day when they're going to leave; they want to get out as quickly as possible. This has been a more recent phenomenon. When I came on the job in 1981, it seemed like everyone had 20 years or more. This was partially due to the fiscal crisis in New York City in the mid-1970s. Thousands of police officers were laid off, and other than the slow process of bringing back the laid off officers, there were no new hirings for a good number of years, resulting in the job getting older. Today, cops come in younger and leave early. The main reason is that pensions have mushroomed as a result of collective bargaining.

What do cops do in this afterlife? How do they prepare for it? Is the afterlife paradise or damnation, or simply a transition to another existence (another job). One thing appears certain – preparation is the key to the afterlife. Those with strong religious beliefs point to the quality of the lives we lead as being the deciding factor in the afterlife. Live a good life – be rewarded in the afterlife.

Live a bad life – face punishment in the afterlife. There is a similar correlation with life after the job. Prepare properly during the career and you are rewarded with an afterlife of post-retirement paradise. Seems easy, right?

I recently read a blog written by a police lieutenant who had been retired for several years. In the blog, he detailed how easy it was for him to attain his post-retirement nirvana. This retiree stated that he prepared financially for his retirement. That was it! That was the only statement on probably the most important factor in a successful afterlife. That statement was similar to me writing that I needed 100K a year to maintain a certain lifestyle, so I went out and obtained a job paying that salary, without any commentary on how I was able to obtain such a job. Anyway, with his financial situation taken care of, the retiree went on to say that long before he retired he planned a number of projects that would keep him busy for several years. He spent a year building an extension on his home and another year writing a book (No, this is not me!). He then spent several years on the road traveling all over the country. There was much more but I could not go further. I was too busy getting sick. I readily admit my illness was generated purely from jealousy. Somehow, my afterlife was quite different from this blogger. I was not sailing into a Caribbean sunset. I was still battling rush hour traffic every day on the Long Island Expressway. Why? I believe, or at least I hope, that my afterlife experience is more the norm. It's not damnation, but I certainly can't call it paradise either. There is something ironic about being "retired", and working harder and longer than during the police career.

Ultimately, as with police work in general, there is something darkly humorous about life after the job. This includes the process of going out the door, as well as some of the crazy things cops do after retirement.

Passing Over

I have never been an overly sentimental person, but on my retirement day even I was touched by the cold, impersonal nature of the process. To be fair, the NYPD is a massive organization with retirements taking place every day. For the personnel processing the retirements, it's just another day at the office.

Only two segments of the day stand out in my memory. First, was the moment I turned in my shield. I handed my captain's shield over to a guy standing behind a counter. He never made eye contact with me as he took the shield and threw it into a box filled with shields. Even for an unsentimental sort such as myself, there was something wrong about tossing the shield into a box. Obviously, I wasn't the only person who felt this way. A couple of years after I retired I discovered that this process had changed. Now, retirees place their shields on top of a ceremonial pillow. I imagine the guy behind the counter waits until the retiree leaves the room before grabbing the shield off the pillow and tossing it in the box. The second part of the process that made an impression with me was the last stop in the day. Since I live within New York City, processing my pistol permit was part of the retirement process. I had to visit the Licensing Division to process my handgun permit paperwork. Up to this point in the process, no one had offered congratulations on a twenty-year career. Now, as I sat next to a desk, while a police administrative aide pecked at the keyboard, I received my first and only well wishes, but it wasn't from the typist or any other person. The desk in front of my position was empty, and there was a chair next to this desk that was directly in front of me. On the rear of this chair, someone had written in white out – *CONGRATULATIONS RETIREE.*

A few years after my retirement, I was offered the opportunity to receive congratulations by something other than a chair. I received a letter inviting me to a retirement ceremony. The NYPD began having monthly retirement ceremonies for those members of the service who retired during the previous month. I guess this is a nice idea, but for me and my unsentimental nature, I crumbled up the invitation and threw it away.

Spinning Plates

Do you remember Eric Brenn, the plate spinner who often performed on the Ed Sullivan Show? Eric Brenn was an amazingly talented performer who came on stage with a stack of dinner plates and a bunch of long poles. He'd set one plate spinning on top of a pole, then another, then another, until a dozen were going at once. Out of the corner of his eye he'd spot a plate starting to slow and wobble, and he'd dash over to it, furiously spinning it up to speed again. Then he'd spot another and run over to spin it up. Now THAT's entertainment. It was also a perfect metaphor for a portion of my afterlife.

If there was a checklist for how NOT to prepare for life after the job, I believe I had every box checked. Granted, some of these factors were out of my control but most were very much within my grasp. The factor I could not control was timing. It would have been nice if my retirement coincided with kids moving out of the house, but that was not to be. My daughter was born when I had nine years on the job and my son came along when I was a twelve-year veteran. The math is obvious. When I was pulling the pin after a twenty-year career I still had private high school and college tuitions to deal with. Add to this the factors that I could have controlled, but didn't – mortgage – second mortgage – credit cards. With my insistence of entering the post-twenty-year afterlife, I transitioned to an existence where I needed to maintain a minimum of the same revenue stream I had while on the job.

Obviously, I had my pension, but that was based on half of my police salary. I needed to work to at least make up the difference, and hopefully to add to the incoming revenue. The first afterlife job I obtained was as an investigator with a major insurance company. I loved this job, and it was probably the closest I came to paradise in the afterlife. I worked out of my home and was given a company car with virtually unlimited use. The cases were interesting, and since I have always liked to write, I never had a problem with the investigative reports. I could basically make my own schedule, and very quickly I had come up with a system where I only needed to go out in the field three days a week and still be able to complete all my assignments. Pretty sweet, right? The pay was descent, but not spectacular, and it did put me at an income level where I needed to be – barely.

With all the free time this job offered, much like the lieutenant blogger I referenced earlier, one would think I would have planned all manner of projects, hobbies, and family events to fill my calendar. Remember, however, I said I was barely at the required income level. With so much free time, I should be able to fit another job in there, shouldn't I? Why should I stop at one extra job? Shouldn't I be able to get another into the mix? Slowly I began getting my plates up on the sticks. Could I spin two or three? Would it be possible to spin even more? Let's see how many plates I was able to spin.

Plate 1: Insurance investigator – the primary job that was the basis for the additional plates

Plate 2: Security Officer – All day Saturday at the corporate office of a Long Island medical supplies distributer. This job involved sitting in the lobby of the corporate office when it was closed. Employees were allowed to come in on Saturday, but for most of the day I just sat undisturbed at the desk. What made this plate so good was the fact that I could bring my insurance company laptop with me. Therefore, I could complete all my investigative reports on Saturday while I was being paid to sit in the lobby.

Plate 3: Insurance investigator job 2 – I hooked up with an Ohio based auto insurer to do some work in the New York area. This company did not write auto policies in New York State, but they needed investigations in the New York City area due to the volume of fraudulent policies they were writing. This company wrote policies in Pennsylvania, where insurance rates are significantly cheaper than in New York City. Unfortunately, there were many New York City residents who were using addresses of friends or relatives in Pennsylvania to obtain a lower rate. This company must have been desperate to get these New York City investigations going. I received a call from the company's director of special investigations and after a five-minute phone interview I was emailed a caseload. This plate spun very nicely. It was very simple to find time to work these auto investigations while I was on the road working my primary insurance investigation job. These auto cases were also simple to work. The question in the overwhelming majority of these auto claims was whether the claimant really lived in Pennsylvania, or whether they had just used a Pennsylvania address to obtain the insurance. Typical of these cases was a New York City teacher who claimed to live in PA, about 120-miles from New York City. The interview with this claimant went something like this:

Q: Do you commute from home in PA to work in NYC every day?

A: Yes

Q: How do you commute?

A: I drive

Q: How long does it take you to get to work?

A: About two and a half hours

Q: Please tell me the specific route you take every day.

A: Well, I leave my house and then, uhhhh............

It was amazing to me what little preparation people would make to support their lie. I guess they just assumed no one would ever ask them anything about their fictitious PA home.

Plate 4: Activity checks – Consolidated Edison, Inc., commonly known as Con Edison or Con Ed is one of the largest energy companies in the United States. The company provides a wide range of energy-related products and services to its customers through its subsidiaries. Consolidated Edison Company of New York provides electric and gas service in New York City and Westchester County. Evidently, there are tons of Con Ed retirees living in the NYC area. I was able to hook up with the company that was contracted by Con Ed to perform activity checks on their pensioners. An activity check simply meant going to the pensioners homes and making sure they were still alive. I would be emailed a list of names and addresses in my area for me to visit. This was another easy plate to spin. My list of Con Ed retirees was geographically clustered close together, so when I would be out on the road conducting the insurance investigations, on the way home I would spend an hour or so calling on Con Ed retirees. And again, I will refer back to plate 2. All my reports – the two insurance companies and the Con Ed activity checks were performed while I was working as a security officer on Saturdays.

Plate 5: Let's see, I had a plate spinning on Saturdays, but the last time I checked there are two days in a weekend. Couldn't I get a plate up there spinning on Sunday's? Maybe not a lesser man, but I was now obsessed. I spent several years during my police career as a police academy instructor. When New York State instituted a security guard licensing law, my police training background made it simple for me to become certified as an instructor to teach the training courses mandated by this licensing law. It was a perfect fit. Most Sunday mornings found me in front of a class of new security guards eager to learn the basics of their new trade. I said most Sunday's, didn't I? That means I still had some available Sunday's, right? On to plate 6.

Plate 6: I became certified to teach the New York State defensive driving course that allows drivers who complete the course to receive a discount on their insurance and/or a point reduction from their license. On the Sunday's I was not in a classroom in front of a room of new security guards, I was in a classroom in front of a group of drivers.

By this time, you have most likely concluded that I am insane – and you are probably correct. I kept these plates spinning for several years after I retired from the NYPD. It actually became something of a game to keep these plates spinning. Eventually, I toned it down, but for some bizarre reason, I look back very fondly on my plate spinning years.

What the Experts Say

With my experience of passing into the police afterlife, I would be the last person to write a book about preparing for retirement and retirement jobs available to police officers. Since I was not up to the task of providing this advice and information, I sought out experts in the field.

The Internet is truly amazing. Sometimes we don't appreciate the full depth of information available at our fingertips. Granted, much of it is completely useless, but sometimes useless information can be attractive when you have nothing to do, and you can't find anything to watch on the hundreds of television channels available. One of my favorite useless information pastimes is looking up online lists. There are lists for anything and everything. I once found Jeffrey Dahmer's jacket and a mummified tongue in a list of the creepiest items for sale on Ebay. I also found that there was a superhero named Cable included in a list of worst superhero costumes. It was clear why Cable made this list, seeing that his costume appeared to be nothing more than a bunch of cables wrapped around him.

A list much more mainstream and suited to my tastes and research was the ten most exciting jobs for retired police officers. I wish I had been Internet savvy enough to be aware of these type lists when I retired. The amazing insights provided very well may have altered my entire post-retirement path. This list couldn't be more of the useless information I was usually bombarded with. After all, the author of the list cited his scientific process for developing this list –

a database of over 7 million resumes. The author looked at all resumes that listed police work under the work history and then looked at which jobs showed up on their work histories following their police positions, sorting them by their most frequent. This man obviously did his homework. I was looking forward to some incredible insights regarding where my post-retirement career could have gone.

Some obvious occupations made the list, such as public safety director and loss prevention specialist. Police officers do tend to remain in the security field upon retirement, but some branch out to other occupations. Barber was on the list. Hmm. I guess that could be an exciting retirement job if you like cutting hair. The author began to lose me when "Agent" was on the list. It was not so much the title that bothered me as it was the description of the occupation. The job was described as either someone who acts as a third party to mediate contracts and relationships between two other parties, or it could be a James Bond-style secret agent. I'm serious - that's how the job was described. The final straw for this list was two particular listed jobs. The first was airline pilot. Obviously, I missed a tremendous opportunity when I retired from the NYPD. If I had only known about this list I would have marched right over to American Airlines and got a job flying their jets. I realize that with my lack of experience I likely would not be able to fly international flights, but I would have been content to fly domestically, at least until I was able to get a pilot's license. The final job on the list of exciting post-retirement careers for police officers was even more absurd - Platoon Sergeant. The description of this potential post-retirement career asserts that experience in police work won't hurt if you are seeking this position. I can see it now. The typical police retiree - a 45-55 overweight male marches into the Army recruiting office and states confidently, "I'm here for the platoon sergeant position. I have an article with me that says my police experience won't hurt." Hell, I retired as a Captain. If I had been aware of this post-retirement career path, maybe I could have become a general.

Afterlife Case Studies

For many NYPD cops, the life after the job dream involves a move to Florida. Police are not unique in this aspect. No state income tax, no inheritance tax or estate tax. That's a big deal, particularly when you are on a fixed income. Why live in a state that is going to tax you when you don't have to? Despite the naysayers who rail about how hot it is in <u>Florida</u>, in the summer months, the average high temperature is 81 degrees Fahrenheit, while the average annual low temperature remains a comfortable 60 degrees Fahrenheit. At the end of the day, if you are on a fixed income, it behooves you to live someplace where your money goes further. Living somewhere that has an average, or below average, cost of living makes sense even if you are one of the lucky ones who was able to save money for retirement. If you live in a place like Florida, your overall cost of living can be lower and you could do other things with your money like travel, spend it on family, or give it to a charity that is important to you. Florida's lower costs, on just about everything, could make a real difference to the monthly budget.

There's no disputing that Florida is an attractive retirement location – just not for me. Self admittedly, my main reason for not moving from the New York City Metropolitan area is also the most ridiculous – it's just too much work. At this stage of my life I'm not going to be pulling up stakes and starting a new life when my old life is dangerously close to entering the home stretch. Additionally, I have no desire to dodge hurricanes every season. That being said, I know several cops who have left New York for the promised land.

One in particular was a cop named Mike. Like many others before and after him, Mike did some preparation for retirement, but even with a move to the Sunshine State's lower cost of living, he couldn't pull off living solely off his pension. Mike still had to work. One of the negative aspects of the move to Florida is the sparsity of jobs, so Mike felt lucky to find employment as a security officer in the local school district. This income put Mike over the top for what he needed to live relatively comfortably, but he was also able to land one of those jobs that everyone talks about but no one ever really gets – that opportunity to use your hobbies as employment.

Mike had two hobbies, both of which he pursued passionately – golf and scuba diving. He was a scratch golfer and he had just about every scuba certification possible. When he got settled in Florida the first thing Mike did was to join the local golf club. Very quickly he got to know the manager of the club, and during one of their conversations the manager detailed a problem he was experiencing. The golf course had three large water hazards, and the manager mentioned to Mike that there were thousands of golf balls at the bottom of these bodies of water, and that it might be worth his while to hire someone to retrieve the balls for resale. Mike did not let this opportunity pass. He pitched his expertise to the manager and was quickly hired by the club to dive once a week to retrieve golf balls. The pay wasn't much, but as a club employee, he now played golf for free. Think about it – a golfer / scuba diver who gets paid to dive for golf balls. Retirement jobs don't get much better than that.

Sgt. Ron knew what he wanted in the afterlife. We were going to retire around the same time, so most of our pre-retirement conversations focused on the afterlife. Ron had one central theme regarding his journey to the great beyond. He was not going to be pigeon holed into the stereotypical police afterlife of private security. Ron was adamant that with his communication and management skills gleaned over twenty years on the job, he would have no problem breaking into the ranks of management in a completely different industry. Shortly after Ron retired he called me and very excitedly said he had been hired as a manager for a tour bus company based near his home on Long Island. He said he would be responsible for maintaining the fleet of buses and scheduling the drivers. Ron was very proud that he was able to break away from the security mold retired cops usually fall into.

About a year and a half after I retired I was attending a professional wrestling event with my son at Madison Square Garden (Wait! Please don't return the book. I've been watching wrestling with my son since he was six years old. Can't a father and son bond?) Anyway, while walking through the corridors of the Garden I run right into Ron. He was not a fan like me – he was working. Ron was a security supervisor at Madison Square Garden. Normally, I'd say Ron scored in the afterlife. The pay was probably pretty good, and I'm sure he had access to all the Garden events. Overall – a pretty good deal. But this was Sgt. Ron who was going to break the mold of the private security paradigm for retired cops. I certainly wasn't going to say anything to Ron about his post-retirement career path, but he must have remembered our pre-retirement conversations and he seemed uncomfortable about being seen in his private security role. Ron volunteered that the tour bus company required that he complete their six-month management training program. He further stated that he fell short of completing the program by five months and twenty-nine days when he discovered that training to be a manager involved pumping out the bus toilets and washing the buses. Suddenly, the private security stereotype didn't seem so bad.

The Afterlife as an Afterlife Job

This look into the afterlife is first-hand information, and actually touches our traditional concept of the afterlife. I met John many years ago while I was a police science instructor at the Police Academy. Cops, like society in general, have diverse political and social views. They have a myriad of different interests and they root for different sports teams. There is one topic, however, in which cops share a universal interest and common bond - the quest to make more money. Cops are always looking for some second front or side gig that will fit into their schedule. So, it was with great interest that I listened to John talk about his newly discovered side job. The academy was running in two squads at the time. This schedule required the recruits and instructors to work Monday - Friday, rotating each week from 8a x 4p to 4p x 12a.

John explained that he had met a guy who was the "Carry Coordinator" for Queens, NY.

My first question was "What is a Carry Coordinator?" John said that most of the funeral homes in the metropolitan area were in some type of coalition that they could reach out to if they needed pall bearers for a funeral. He explained that he received $25 a carry (this was the late 1980s) John went on to say that this was a perfect side gig on the week our academy squad was working 4 x 12, as he could have as many as three carries during a morning, and still have plenty of time to get ready for work. When John mentioned that his contact was looking for additional carriers in Queens, my response was an enthusiastic "Sign me up!"

I received a call from the carry coordinator a few days later and he stated the only requirement to begin carrying was to have a black suit. I have gone through life owning one suit at a time, and at that stage my suit was blue. If I had to invest money into a black suit, how could I make this investment without needing months of carries to break even? My college economics 101 professor would have been proud. I visited a local Salvation Army thrift shop, and for the total sum of $12 I left with a black suit jacket, black dress pants, a white dress shirt, and a black tie, all of which fit me (well, not quite but close enough).

The job was simple enough. For a 9AM funeral mass I would arrive outside the church at 8:45 and meet the other pall bearers. When the hearse pulled up, we would put on our game faces and carry the coffin into the church. Once the coffin was at the front of the church we would hang out outside the church until the end of the mass, when we would carry the coffin out and back into the hearse. That was it. All in all, a single carry job involved about three minutes of actual work, but you did have to hang around during the mass, making the total time commitment for one carry a little over one hour.

Even in the coffin carrying business I quickly discovered that politics played a big role. The people who really did well with this job were the ones who got multiple carries during multiple days. A pall bearer who did three carries a day for three days during the week made $225 - not bad money at that time for working three mornings. On the other hand, the politically unconnected pall bearers like myself, would usually get two carries a week on different days. And to make matters worse, I was usually getting the 11AM carry, so, my whole morning was shot for the sake of one $25 carry. Approximately 6-months after beginning my part time carrying career we went to a different duty chart at the police academy enabling me to gracefully bow out of the coffin carrying business. I resolved that the next time I would be involved in a carry would be when I was inside the coffin.

There was a very weird postscript to this very brief part time career. Approximately ten years after my last carry I was now a captain, sitting at home one early evening enjoying the television. I answered the phone and the conversation went something like this
"Hey Bob, can you go to Holy Family tomorrow at 9?"
"What?"
"Holy Family tomorrow"
"What about Holy Family?"
"Can you be there at 9 tomorrow?"
"Why?"
"For a carry"
"Carry what? Who is this?"
"It's Jack Gannon," the voice stated with a tone indicating that it was unbelievable that I didn't know who he was.

Jack Gannon was the carry coordinator PO John had hooked me up with ten years earlier. I had not heard from this man in ten years, and out of the blue he calls to see if I can do a carry the next day. Who knows? If I still had my Salvation Army black suit, I might have done it.

I know what you're asking yourself about now. What does my brief coffin carrying side gig have to do with the retirement afterlife? In a script that I could not have written better, a few years after I retired I met PO John at - where else? - the wake of a retired cop. John told me that after he retired he took over for Jack Gannon and was now the Carry Coordinator. The experts who say that you should always be ready to network are absolutely right, because right outside that funeral parlor, John offered me the opportunity to get back into the carrying business. You may find this hard to believe, but I turned down this tremendous opportunity without even finding out what the present pay rate for a carry was. John would not be deterred. He attempted to hook me with another opportunity that I did not know existed. He wanted to know if I wanted to be on his "Mourner" list. "What?" As ridiculous as this may seem, there are times when loved ones of the deceased believe it's important to fill the church with mourners, but they know they will come up short with actual friends and family. The solution - call a mourner. I did not even want to know the pay rate for professional mourner. This was just too depressing, but if I found out the pay was good I probably would have done it.

The Merry Mailman

When I was a rookie the standard advice offered by salty veterans was "Do your twenty, kid, and get out." I'm sure similar guidance is offered today, although the NYPD no longer has a twenty-year retirement. During the recommendations I received, however, the majority of the times there was a second piece of advice. Not only was I urged to get out at twenty, but I was given a recommendation to a new career – the Post Office.

The concept of a second career with the Post Office made sense – to a degree. There are limitations as to where a retired police officer can seek employment in the afterlife. If a cop wants to begin collecting his/her pension immediately after retirement (who doesn't?) the cop has to be careful not to illegally "double-dip."

According to the New York City Charter, the pension portion of the retirement benefit is suspended or forfeited for all retired persons who are employed by New York State or any of its political subdivisions and earn over $1,800.00 per year. However, Section 211 of the New York State Retirement and Social Security Law allows a person retired for other than physical disability to be employed by New York State or one of its political subdivisions if the agency wishing to employ the person obtains approval from the New York State Civil Service Commission or others empowered to grant such approval. This is commonly known as the "211 waiver." In addition, if the prospective employer is New York City (except the NYC Department of Education), the salary or compensation is limited to the difference between the yearly pension amount and the current salary or compensation the pension was based on. Earnings in excess of that amount will result in the recoupment of overpayment. Section 212 of the New York State Retirement and Social Security Law permits employment by New York State or one of its political subdivisions without approval for non-disability-retired persons if the salary or compensation is less than an amount set by State legislature each year (currently $30,000). Under Section 212, you must notify the Police Pension Fund in writing if you intend to exercise this right.

What does all this gibberish mean? Very simply, after retirement NYPD cops are prohibited from working for a City, State, or local municipality without obtaining one of the aforementioned waivers. The only exception to this waiver requirement were agencies designated as Public Benefit Corporations, such as the New York City Transit Authority, Housing Authority, and Health & Hospitals Corporation.

So, why the recommendation for the Post Office? The restriction on government employment does not apply to federal agencies. A retiree could get a post-retirement job with any federal agency without the need of any waiver. There are numerous law enforcement agencies within the federal government. Wouldn't a retired cop be better suited for a federal law enforcement job rather than the Post office? Herein lies another retirement fly in the ointment. Of course, retired police officers would be highly qualified for federal law enforcement work. Most federal law enforcement jobs, however, have a maximum age limit of 35 to enter the agency. Retired cops completing a minimum of twenty years on the job would be well over this age limit. This brings us full circle back to the Post Office – a federal job with no age restrictions. But I didn't want to be a mailman as a first career. Why would I want to be a letter carrier in a second career?

To an extent, I drank the cool aid. With about six months until requirement I sat for the city carrier postal exam. I've always been a pretty good test taker and I did well on this test. Shortly after I retired I received a letter offering me employment with the post office. My first emotion was elation. I had done it. I had been able to bring reality to the advice and recommendations given to me twenty years earlier. Very quickly, however, elation transitioned into confusion. Why was I so happy? I never had any desire to be a mailman twenty years ago, and I surely had not developed an urge over the years to roam the streets with a mailbag. So, I turned down a second career as the merry mailman. I'm sure there are plenty of retired cops who have had fruitful second careers with the Post Office – I just don't know of any.

Police Officer Jim is typical of the cops I knew who turned in their shield for a mail sack. Jim had fifteen years on the job when I was a rookie, and for the five years that we worked in the same command I cannot remember one conversation with Jim that did not involve his goal to work at the Post Office. Jim made his twenty years and retired, hopefully to a happy ending with the Postal

Service. About five years after Jim retired, my partner Rick moved to Staten Island. The first time Rick visited his local Post Office, who do you think was the clerk behind the counter? You guessed it – Jim. So, this retirement story had a happy ending, right? Well, maybe not so fast. When Rick entered the Post Office, Jim was screaming at several of the customers on line. When Jim recognized Rick, he went into a diatribe of how the management sucks, his co-workers suck, and the customers suck. Every subsequent time Rick entered that Post Office, Jim was in the midst of some type of confrontation with a supervisor or customer. So much for his happy ending.

Honestly, I don't know of any retired cops who had a positive experience working for the Post Office. The closest to anything positive was a bizarre story I heard many years ago. When I was a rookie I heard a story about the Postal Strike of 1970. The eight-day strike began in New York City and spread to some other cities in the following two weeks. This strike against the federal government, regarded as illegal, was the largest wildcat strike in U.S. history.

President Nixon called out the National Guard in an attempt to distribute the mail and break the strike. Lieutenant Louie was a cop at the time and a member of the National Guard. He was activated to postal duty and was subsequently injured when he was struck in the head with a mailbag. Somehow, this injury was enough to grant him status as a disabled veteran. The significance of this designation was additional points awarded on civil service exams, such as Louie's exams for sergeant and lieutenant. As the story reached mythical proportions, some versions had Louie receiving a Purple Heart Medal. I'm certain that was not true – I think.

The Longevity Penalty

The goal for most people is to live a long, healthy life. For police officers who retire at a very young age, there can be a paradox in play. That long, healthy life can result in a longevity penalty.

I mentioned in my plate spinning endeavors, that one of my many retirement jobs was teaching classes for people taking the required training to obtain a New York State Security Guard License. Well, I never went cold turkey with my plate spinning, and I still occasionally teach these classes. Several months ago, I had a perfect example of the longevity penalty in my class. Jerry was 73-years old and was retired from a Nassau County village police department. Jerry had come on the job when he was twenty-one years old and retired after twenty years at the ripe old age of forty-one. At the time of his retirement, Jerry was single and he immediately moved to Florida and lived a carefree, workfree lifestyle. He was a self-proclaimed man of leisure, doing whatever he felt like whenever he felt like doing it. As the years went by, the lack of any meaningful cost of living raises ate into his pension, but he still had no problem maintaining his lifestyle. When he turned sixty, he made two decisions that altered his life forever. First, he met a woman and got married, and second, at his wife's insistence, they moved back to the expensive, heavily taxed Long Island region of New York. His wife worked a clerical job and Jerry desperately tried to go on without having to work. His pension could only support his new life for so long. So, here was Jerry, sitting in my class at 73-years of age, after not working for 32-years, learning how to obtain a security guard license. Why? Because he had to! A lot of people won't get this, but this is one of the most frightening stories I have ever heard.

Man with a Plan

Another terrible retirement story is the case of PO Eddie. Eddie and I were both transit cops detailed as instructors to the NYPD Police Academy. At the time I met Eddie he had substantially more time on the job than me. I only had a little over five years on while Eddie had fourteen years on the job. Eddie was a man with a plan. He had a wife and two young daughters and he had fallen in love with a town in Virginia. He was so enamored with Virginia that he bought a home there. Wait! I know what you're thinking. How did Eddie commute to work in New York City from Virginia? As I said, he was a man with a plan.

The academy was operating in two squads, with the recruits and instructors flip flopping week to week from 8am x 4pm shifts to 4pm to 12am tours of duty. Classes were Monday through Friday, so everyone had the weekends off. Regardless of what his schedule called for, Eddie had arranged to work a day tour every Friday and a 4x12 shift each Monday. Friday at 4pm Eddie tore out of the Police Academy and was on the road to Virginia. He could stay with his family the entire weekend, returning to New York City in time for his 4pm shift on Monday. What about during the week? Eddie must have rented an apartment in the city? Not quite. Rent did not fall into Eddie's financial plan, so he took a much simpler path. He lived in the Police Academy during the week. Eddie showered in the locker room and slept, ate and watched TV in the instructor's lounge.

Eddie's plan was to keep this up for a full year and the retire to Virginia. He wouldn't receive the full twenty-year retirement benefit, but at the fifteen-year mark, police officers could "Vest" and retire with a smaller pension benefit.

I was promoted to sergeant and left the academy before Eddie's year of commuting to Virginia was over. I found out a couple of years later that his plan didn't turn out the way he expected. Shortly before reaching his fifteenth anniversary, his wife divorced him. Oh, well, how does that saying go? The best laid plans of mice and men oft go awry – you get the picture.

Before you shed too may tears for Eddie, I learned a bizarre postscript to this story. In my current, and hopefully final retirement job, I met a lady who used to be a police administrative aide with the Transit Police and NYPD. Turns out she became wife number two for Eddie. Eddie completed his twenty years and after retiring he got a job as a cemetery caretaker. Eddie and his wife lived rent free in a big house on top of a hill in the cemetery. The happy couple bought a house together in Florida and planned to live there after a few more years in the cemetery. So, why was this woman typing in my building years later. It seems that without warning, Eddie took off for parts unknown. When his wife checked to see if he went to the Florida house, she was stunned to find that there was no Florida house. Eddie had managed to sell the house without her knowledge. I never heard anything more regarding Eddie. Is he back in the cemetery permanently? Who knows?

The Greatest Retirement Perk

In my current retirement job, I am the Chief Security Officer at a New York State government facility. From time to time I have vacancies in my department, and since the positions are armed, they are ideally suited for retired police officers. Whenever a position comes open the job vacancy is posted for several weeks before I begin interviewing. I will usually receive approximately two hundred resumes per vacancy, so after the resumes are narrowed down to those candidates who meet the qualifications for the position, the interview process will be conducted over several weeks.

During one of these periods I interviewed a retired NYPD detective named George, and as the interview progressed we began talking about different aspects of the job, including retirement jobs. George had been retired a little over two years, and he said that his first retirement job was working on the security detail of a very wealthy, famous man. I knew about cops retiring to work for this guy and I also heard that the pay was exceptional. Nothing is perfect, however, as I also heard that the guy was extremely difficult to work for. George substantiated both details. He said the pay was great, but he told a story that happened to someone he worked with to illustrate just how difficult it was to work for this man.

George said that Michael was also a retired detective, and that one day, Michael was assigned to drive the client in Manhattan. The client carried a portable walkie-talkie radio, and at some point during the drive, Michael apparently failed to follow some instruction, so the client leaned forward in the back seat and whacked Michael hard on the back of the head with the radio. Michael stopped the car – got out – opened the back door and tried to get at the client, while the client slid to the other side of the backseat and began kicking at Michael.

According to George, Michael then made a brilliant move. He stopped trying to get at the client and departed the area on foot. His head was bleeding so he walked into the emergency room of a nearby hospital to be treated. Before he was released from the hospital, representatives of the client appeared in the emergency room to try to smooth over the situation. If George is accurate, Michael got college tuition paid for both his kids to forget about the whole incident. I should only have been so lucky to take a crack in the head.

There's No Place like Home

Lieutenant W. had done it! He had beaten the odds and accomplished the goal most cops find unobtainable. He had retired from the job with his finances in a state where he would never have to work again. For Lt. W. to reach such a milestone, there were some concessions. His career path was not twenty years – it was in excess of forty years.

Lt. W. had been the senior lieutenant on the Transit Police Department for many years. He came on the job when he was twenty-one years old and made lieutenant when he had about nine years on the job. He was a lieutenant for over thirty-three years when New York State law required him to retire on his 63rd birthday. Here's where the story becomes interesting (or strange).

For the purposes of maximizing his pension, Lt. W. had played his hand expertly. Think about it. He had forty-two years on the job with thirty-three of them at the rank of lieutenant. His monthly check was going to be enormous. But maybe his actions were not all part of an ingenious retirement plan. Maybe, Lt. W. had no desire to retire, but only left the job because New York State law forced him to. How can I say that?

I was told by several sources that Lt. W. was able to withhold from his wife the information regarding forced retirement at age sixty-three. Although he had no desire or need to work a retirement job, evidently, Lt. W's idea of a blissful retirement was not spending day after day at home with his wife. But he had to retire, so how did he address this problem? Simple! He simply neglected to inform his wife that he retired. Every day he departed home as he had for many years, only now, he had to find things to do before going home eight hours later. From what I was told by someone who actually talked to Lt. W., the nice weather was easy. He could take a long walk or sit in a park and feed the pigeons. There was more of a challenge during the bad weather, but if conditions were too bad, he always had the option of telling his wife he was calling in sick.

Today, Lt. W. would be well into his eighties, and I believe he is still alive. Is he still leaving his home every day telling his wife he is going to work? Who knows? Those of you who think this story is ridiculous, read it again after you've been married for around forty years. It may not seem so ridiculous anymore.

Do You Miss the Job?

This is without a doubt the question I get asked most frequently once people find out I'm retired from the NYPD. The answer is not a simple yes of no – it's more complicated than you might think.

I was recently talking with Joe, a former sergeant who retired a couple of years after I did. The subject of missing the job came up, and I believe Joe summed it up brilliantly. He said, "Of course I miss the job. What's not to miss. I loved it all, especially the duty captain rolling up on me just as I got a hot cup of coffee on a freezing day and writing me up. I miss working all the holidays. I miss working a rotating schedule and not knowing what day I'm off. I especially miss Times Square on New Year's Eve, and dealing with the drunk kids from the suburbs on St. Patrick's Day. I miss sitting on a DOA (dead body), waiting an eternity for the morgue wagon to arrive. I miss dealing with filthy homeless guys and EDPs (emotionally Disturbed Persons). I miss the rat-infested locker rooms and bathrooms. I miss the monthly activity reports and the summons quotas. I miss the civilian complaints, the denied days off, the CDs (command disciplines). Most of all I miss the police brutality protests and all the public support we receive. Of course, I miss the job – who wouldn't"

Joe's eloquent response captured the essence of the only thing I miss about the job. I miss the brutal, dark humor that is inherent in America's dark knights.

From the Author

Thank you for purchasing DARK KNIGHTS 3. I hope you enjoyed it. This book completes the Dark Knights trilogy.

DARK KNIGHTS was the first in the series and followed my career in the NYC Transit Police and NYPD through a series of darkly funny stories about my experiences and the characters I met during my career.

https://www.amazon.com/dp/B0711CB8K2

DARK KNIGHTS 2 is a humorous account of the two years I spent as a Border Patrol Agent prior to my NYPD career.

https://www.amazon.com/dp/B07GZ6DWTJ

Made in the USA
Columbia, SC
14 February 2021